D0922139

Table of Contents

Using Everyday Comprehension Intervention Activities

Reading with full text comprehension is the ultimate goal of all reading instruction. Students who read the words but don't comprehend them aren't really reading at all. Research has shown that explicit comprehension strategy instruction helps students understand and remember what they read, which allows them to communicate what they've learned with others and perform better in testing situations.

Although some students master comprehension strategies easily during regular classroom instruction, many others need additional re-teaching opportunities to master these essential strategies. The Everyday Intervention Activities series provides easy-to-use, five-day intervention units for Grades K–5. These units are structured around a research-based Model-Guide-Practice-Apply approach. You can use these activities in a variety of intervention models, including Response to Intervention (RTI).

Getting Started

In just five simple steps, Everyday Comprehension Intervention Activities provides everything you need to identify students' comprehension needs and to provide targeted, research-based intervention.

Everyday Comprehension ervention Activities Grade 5 • ©2010 Newmark Learning, LLC

1. PRE-ASSESS to identify students' comprehension needs.

Use the pre-assessment on the CD-ROM to identify the strategies your students need to master.

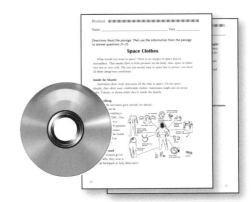

2. MODEL the strategy.

Every five-day unit targets a specific strategy. On Day 1, use the teacher prompts and reproducible activity to introduce and model the strategy.

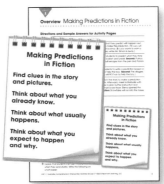

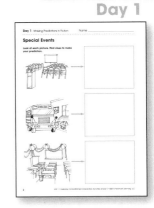

Day 1

3. GUIDE PRACTICE and APPLY.

Use the reproducible practice activities for Days 2, 3, and 4 to build students' understanding of, and proficiency with, the strategy.

Day 2

Day 3

Day 4

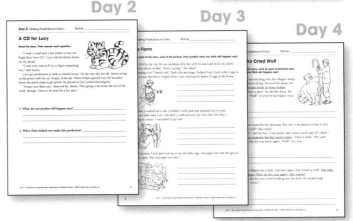

4. MONITOR progress.

Administer the Day 5 reproducible assessment to monitor each student's progress and to make instructional decisions.

Day 5

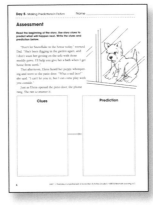

5. POST-ASSESS to document student progress.

Use the post-assessment on the CD-ROM to measure students' progress as a result of your interventions.

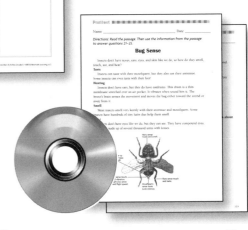

Standards-Based Comprehension Strategies in Everyday Intervention Activities

The comprehension strategies found in the Everyday Intervention Activities series are introduced developmentally and spiral from one grade to the next based on curriculum standards across a variety of states. The chart below shows the comprehension strategies addressed at each grade level in this series.

Comprehension Strategy	Strategy Definition	K	1	2	3	4	5
Make Predictions	Determine what might happen next in a story or nonfiction piece. Predictions are based on information presented in the text.	✔	✔	✔	✔	✔	✔
Identify Sequence of Events	Determine the order of events for topics such as history, science, or biography. Determine the steps to make or do something.	✔	✔	✔	✔	✔	✔
Analyze Story Elements	Analyze the setting and plot (problem/solution) in a fiction text.	✔	✔	✔	✔	✔	✔
Analyze Character	Analyze story characters based on information and on clues and evidence in the text, including description, actions, dialogue, feelings, and traits.	✔	✔	✔	✔	✔	✔
Identify Main Idea and Supporting Details	Determine what the paragraph, page, or chapter is mostly about. Sometimes the main idea is stated and sometimes it is implied. Students must choose details that support the main idea, not "just any detail."	✔	✔	✔	✔	✔	✔
Summarize	Take key ideas from the text and put them together to create a shorter version of the original text. Summaries should have few, if any, details.	✔	✔	✔	✔	✔	✔
Compare and Contrast	Find ways that two things are alike and different.	✔	✔	✔	✔	✔	✔
Identify Cause and Effect	Find things that happened (effect) and why they happened (cause). Text may contain multiple causes and effects.	✔	✔	✔	✔	✔	✔
Make Inferences	Determine what the author is suggesting without directly stating it. Inferences are usually made during reading and are made from one or two pieces of information from the text. Students' inferences will vary but must be made from the evidence in the text and background knowledge.	✔	✔	✔	✔	✔	✔
Draw Conclusions	Determine what the author is suggesting without directly stating it. Conclusions are made during and after reading, and are made from multiple (3+) pieces of information from the text. Students' conclusions will vary but must be drawn from the evidence in the text and background knowledge.		✔	✔	✔	✔	✔
Evaluate Author's Purpose	Determine why the author wrote the passage or used certain information. A book can have more than one purpose. Purposes include to entertain, to inform, and to persuade.			✔	✔	✔	✔
Analyze Text Structure and Organization	Determine the text structure to better understand what the author is saying and to use as research when text must be analyzed.			✔	✔	✔	✔
Use Text Features to Locate Information	Use text features (bullets, captions, glossary, index, sidebars) to enhance meaning.			✔	✔	✔	✔
Use Graphic Features to Interpret Information	Use clues from graphic features (charts, maps, graphs) to determine what is not stated in the text or to enhance meaning.			✔	✔	✔	✔
Distinguish and Evaluate Facts and Opinions	Recognize objective statements of fact and subjective opinions within a nonfiction text.					✔	✔
Make Judgments	Use facts from the text and prior knowledge and beliefs to make and confirm opinions about the characters or situations.					✔	✔

Everyday Comprehension Intervention Activities Grade 5 • ©2010 Newmark Learning, LLC

Using Everyday Intervention for RTI

According to the National Center on Response to Intervention, RTI "integrates assessment and intervention within a multi-level prevention system to maximize student achievement and to reduce behavior problems." This model of instruction and assessment allows schools to identify at-risk students, monitor their progress, provide research-proven interventions, and "adjust the intensity and nature of those interventions depending on a student's responsiveness."

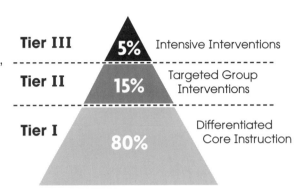

RTI models vary from district to district, but the most prevalent model is a three-tiered approach to instruction and assessment.

The Three Tiers of RTI	Using Everyday Intervention Activities
Tier I: Differentiated Core Instruction • Designed for all students • Preventive, proactive, standards-aligned instruction • Whole- and small-group differentiated instruction • Ninety-minute, daily core reading instruction in the five essential skill areas: phonics, phonemic awareness, comprehension, vocabulary, fluency	• Use whole-group comprehension mini-lessons to introduce and guide practice with comprehension strategies that all students need to learn. • Use any or all of the units in the order that supports your core instructional program.
Tier II: Targeted Group Interventions • For at-risk students • Provide thirty minutes of daily instruction beyond the ninety-minute Tier I core reading instruction • Instruction is conducted in small groups of three to five students with similar needs	• Select units based on your students' areas of need (the pre-assessment can help you identify these). • Use the units as week-long, small-group mini-lessons.
Tier III: Intensive Interventions • For high-risk students experiencing considerable difficulty in reading • Provide up to sixty minutes of additional intensive intervention each day in addition to the ninety-minute Tier I core reading instruction • More intense and explicit instruction • Instruction conducted individually or with smaller groups of one to three students with similar needs	• Select units based on your students' areas of need. • Use the units as one component of an intensive comprehension intervention program.

Overview Making Predictions in Fiction

Directions and Sample Answers for Activity Pages

Day 1	See "Provide a Real-World Example" below.
Day 2	Read and discuss the story. Ask students to write what they predict will happen next. Then ask them to write the clues that helped them make this prediction. (**1:** Lucy will earn money for playing with Stripes while Mr. Simon is away. **2:** Lucy wants to earn a few dollars. Stripes likes Lucy. He's going to be lonely while Mr. Simon is away.)
Day 3	Read and discuss each part of the story. Then ask students to predict what they think will happen next. (**First:** The eggs will spill from the basket and break. **Second:** Patrick will go walking somewhere else. **Third:** The piglet will escape from the pen and Patrick will try to catch it.)
Day 4	Read each part of the story together. Then ask students to write a prediction based on the underlined clues. (**First:** The villagers will run to help the boy. **Second:** The villagers will run to help the boy again. **Third:** The villagers will NOT run to help the boy.)
Day 5	Read the story together. Ask students to use clues in the story to make a prediction and record their ideas on their graphic organizers. Afterward, meet individually with students to discuss their results. Use their responses to plan further instruction and review. (**Clues:** Snowflake was whimpering. She had a sad face. Elena opened the patio door. She ran to answer the phone. **Prediction:** Snowflake will run into the house and get on the sofa.)

Provide a Real-World Example

◆ Hand out the Day 1 activity page.

◆ **Say:** *Sometimes a class participates in special events at school. We can often predict, or make a good guess, that a special event is about to happen.*

◆ Ask students to look at the first picture. **Ask:** *What clues do you see that a special event is about to happen? What do you already know about these clues? What special event do you predict the class will participate in?*

◆ Allow time for students to write their predictions in the blank box and share them with the group. For example, they might predict that the class will listen to a guest speaker.

◆ Repeat the process with the remaining pictures (class field trip, class party). Invite students to share their predictions. **Ask:** *What clues did you use? What do you already know that helped you make your prediction?*

◆ Explain that students can also make predictions when they read stories. Write the following on chart paper:

Making Predictions in Fiction

Find clues in the story and pictures.

Think about what you already know.

Think about what usually happens.

Think about what you expect to happen and why.

Special Events

Look at each picture. Find clues to make your prediction.

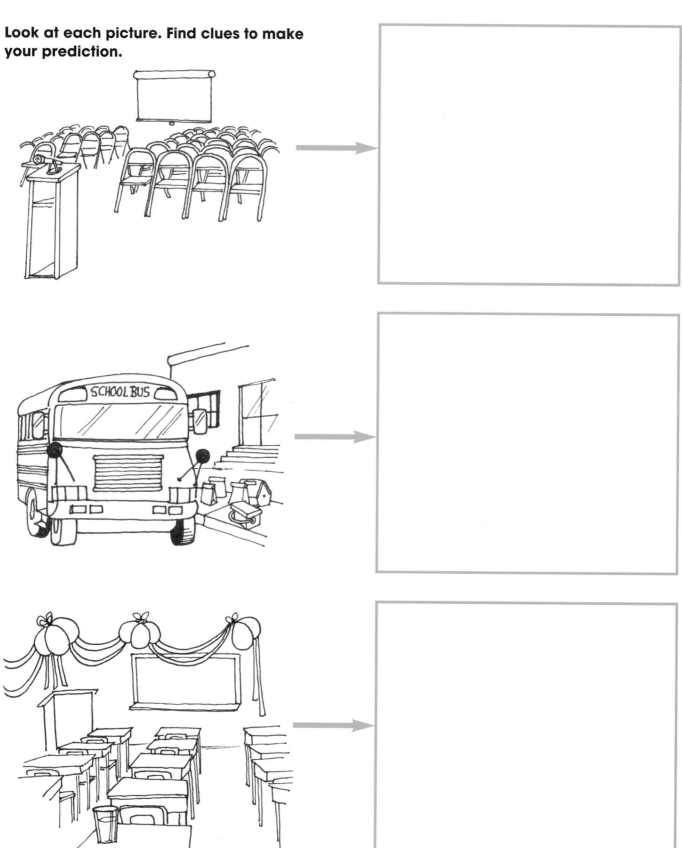

A CD for Lucy

Read the story. Then answer each question.

"I wish I could earn a few dollars to buy the Bugle Boys' new CD," Lucy told her friend Azaria on the phone.

"Come over, and we'll try to figure something out," said Azaria.

Lucy got permission to walk to Azaria's house. On the way, she saw Mr. Simon sitting on his porch with his cat, Stripes, in his lap. When Stripes spotted Lucy, he bounded down the porch steps to get petted. He purred as Lucy stroked his long fur.

"Stripes sure likes you," observed Mr. Simon. "He's going to be lonely the rest of the week, though. I have to be away for a few days."

1. **What do you predict will happen next?** _____

_____

_____

2. **What clues helped you make this prediction?** _____

_____

_____

On the Farm

Read each part of the story. Look at the picture.
Then predict what you think will happen next.

Patrick lived in the city. He was spending a few days with his aunt and uncle on a farm. Mom called to check on him. "How's it going?" she asked.

"I'm learning a lot!" Patrick said. "Early this morning, I helped Aunt Carol collect eggs in the chicken coop. But then I tripped when I was carrying the basket of eggs to the house."

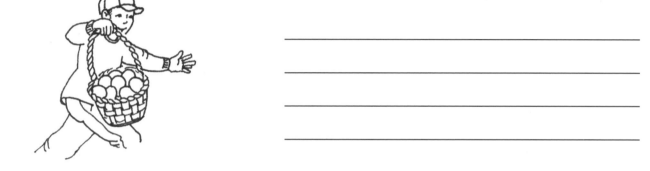

_____
_____
_____
_____

"After that, I walked out to the cornfield. Uncle Jack sure planted a lot of corn! The stalks are taller than I am. I decided to walk between the rows, but I felt like I was walking in a maze. I was afraid I'd get lost!"

_____
_____
_____
_____

"This afternoon, Uncle Jack took me to see the baby pigs. One piglet saw that the gate to the pen was open. Was that piglet ever fast!"

_____
_____
_____
_____

The Boy Who Cried Wolf

**Read each part of the story. Look at each underlined clue.
Then predict what you think will happen next.**

A shepherd boy was watching over the villagers' sheep.
He loved being outdoors all day. He loved the sheep, too.
But soon, <u>the boy became lonely for some human
companionship</u>. "I have a plan!" he told the sheep. He
took a deep breath. "Wolf!" he cried in his loudest voice.

My prediction: _____

_____

When the villagers heard the boy shouting, they ran to the pasture as fast as they
could. "Where's the wolf?" they asked.

"Uh . . . nowhere," said the boy. "I was lonely, and I knew you'd come if I called."
<u>The villagers were surprised, but they weren't upset</u>. "That's a relief!" they said.
A few days later, the boy was lonely again. "Wolf!" he cried.

My prediction: _____

_____

Once again, the villagers ran to help. And once again, they found no wolf. <u>This time,
the villagers were angry. "Don't try this trick again!" they warned</u>.

A few days later, the boy saw a wolf sneaking into the flock. He needed help!
"WOLF!" he cried. "WOLF!"

My prediction: _____

_____

Assessment

Read the beginning of the story. Use story clues to predict what will happen next. Write the clues and prediction below.

"Don't let Snowflake in the house today," warned Dad. "She's been digging in the garden again, and I don't want her getting on the sofa with those muddy paws. I'll help you give her a bath when I get home from work."

That afternoon, Elena heard her puppy whimpering and went to the patio door. "What a sad face!" she said. "I can't let you in, but I can come play with you outside."

Just as Elena opened the patio door, the phone rang. She ran to answer it.

Clues	**Prediction**

Overview Making Predictions in Nonfiction

Directions and Sample Answers for Activity Pages

Day 1	See "Provide a Real-World Example" below.
Day 2	Read the recipe and baking tips together. Then ask students to circle the best predictions. (**1:** The cake will still taste like chocolate cake. **2:** The cake will still taste good. **3:** The cake could dry out a little.)
Day 3	Read and discuss the passage. Then ask students to answer the questions. (**1:** The green sea turtle might become extinct. **2:** Hunters kill the turtles and sell the eggs; some get trapped in fishing nets; some are injured or killed by boat propellers; humans destroy habitats when they build.)
Day 4	Read and discuss the passage together. Then ask students to color the circle in front of the best prediction and each piece of evidence. (**1:** Both players will win approximately the same number of games. **2:** Each person hammers a fist into the palm of the other hand twice. Each person chooses to make a rock, scissors, or paper on the third hammer. Either rock, scissors, or paper might win the game.)
Day 5	Read the passage together. Ask students to use the evidence in the passage to make a prediction and record their ideas on their graphic organizers. Afterward, meet individually with students to discuss their results. Use their responses to plan further instruction and review. (**Evidence:** muscles get stronger; lungs become stronger; heart pumps faster; brain gets more oxygen; feel good; learn and remember things better. **Prediction:** I will be healthier.)

Provide a Real-World Example

◆ Hand out the Day 1 activity page.

◆ **Say:** *My friend loves to visit her grandchildren on weekends. Once I called her on a Saturday to ask about borrowing a book. When she didn't answer the phone, I predicted—or made a good guess—that she was spending the day with her grandchildren. I used what I know about my friend as evidence to make my prediction.*

◆ Ask students to look at their activity page. Then have them Think/Pair/Share other predictions you could have made.

◆ Pair students. Ask them to use what they know about each other to predict what their partner might do this Saturday. After a student writes a prediction, the partner should either confirm it or give additional clues to help the student make a more accurate prediction.

◆ Explain that students can also make predictions when they read. Write the following on chart paper:

Making Predictions in Nonfiction

Find evidence in the passage and pictures.

Think about what you already know.

Think about what usually happens.

Think about what you expect to happen and why.

Saturday

Listen. Then make other possible predictions.

One Prediction:
I predict that my friend is spending
the day with her grandchildren.

Other predictions:
I predict that _____ .

What will your partner do on Saturday?
Use what you know to make predictions.

1. I predict that _____
will _____
this Saturday.

2. _____ My partner confirmed my prediction.

3. _____ My partner will give me more clues,
and then I will revise my prediction.

4. I predict that _____ will _____
_____ this Saturday.

Chocolate Cake

Read the cake recipe and cake baking tips. Then circle the best answer to each question.

Chocolate Cake

1 4-ounce bar sweet cooking chocolate

½ cup butter

1 cup sugar

3 eggs

1 teaspoon vanilla

⅔ cup buttermilk

1¾ cups flour

Melt chocolate bar and let it cool.

Cream the butter and sugar together. Add melted chocolate, eggs, vanilla, and buttermilk. Stir in flour. Bake at 350 degrees for 25 to 30 minutes.

Cake Baking Tips: If you don't have one of the ingredients on hand, you can either choose another recipe or substitute a similar ingredient. You may also leave out an ingredient if its only purpose is to add a bit of flavoring. When a recipe gives a range for the baking time, start with the lower number of minutes and then bake a little longer if needed.

1. **What do you predict may happen if the baker substitutes cocoa for the chocolate bar?**

   The cake will still taste like chocolate cake.

   The baker will decide to choose another recipe.

2. **What do you predict may happen if the baker leaves out the vanilla?**

   The cake will be ruined.

   The cake will still taste good.

3. **What do you predict may happen if the baker bakes the cake for 30 minutes?**

   The baker will forget to take it out of the oven.

   The cake could dry out a little.

Giant Sea Turtles

Read the passage. Then answer each question.

Green sea turtles weigh between 400 and 500 pounds. This giant turtle has few enemies. Sharks and humans are its main predators. Even though many countries have laws against killing the "greens," some turtle hunters ignore the laws. These hunters kill the turtles and sell the meat, skin, and oil. They dig up the turtles' eggs and sell them, too. The green sea turtle population is also shrinking because of accidents. Some greens get trapped in fishing nets and drown, and others are injured or killed by boat propellers. Humans destroy the greens' habitats when they build. The construction often pollutes the water and disturbs the turtles' nests.

1. What do you predict might happen? _____

_____

2. What evidence helps you make this prediction? _____

_____

Probability

Read the passage.

Have you ever played the game Rock, Paper, Scissors? First, choose a partner. Each of you will hammer the side of your fist into the palm of your other hand twice. On the third hammer, you either leave your hand in a fist (rock), extend all your fingers to form a flat surface (paper), or extend your index and middle fingers into a V shape (scissors). If you both choose the same formation, the game is a tie. If you choose different formations, score as follows:

- Rock/Scissors (The rock wins, because a rock can crush scissors.)
- Scissors/Paper (Scissors win, because scissors can cut paper.)
- Paper/Rock (Paper wins, because paper can wrap up a rock.)

Try the game with a friend. Keep a tally of who wins each game. Who do you predict will win the most games?

1. Color the circle in front of the best prediction.

○ The player who chooses a rock the most often will probably win the most games.

○ The player who chooses scissors the most often will probably win the most games.

○ The player who chooses paper the most often will probably win the most games.

○ Both players will win approximately the same number of games.

2. Color the circle in front of each piece of evidence from the passage.

○ Each person hammers a fist into the palm of the other hand twice.

○ Each person chooses to make a rock, scissors, or paper on the third hammer.

○ Rock wins more than scissors.

○ Scissors wins more than paper.

○ Paper wins more than rock.

○ Either rock, scissors, or paper might win the game.

Assessment

Read the passage. Use evidence from the passage to predict what may happen later. Write the evidence and prediction below.

Exercise is movement. You get some exercise naturally as you go about your day. But many people like to get additional exercise, such as biking, dancing, or playing a sport. This exercise has many benefits for your body. For example, when you run, your leg and arm muscles get stronger. Your lungs become stronger, too. As you breathe harder, you take in more oxygen, which your lungs then send to your blood. At the same time, your heart pumps faster and circulates the blood to help your muscles get the energy they need. Even your brain gets more oxygen, which makes you feel good and helps you learn and remember things better. What could happen if you start adding more exercise to YOUR daily routine?

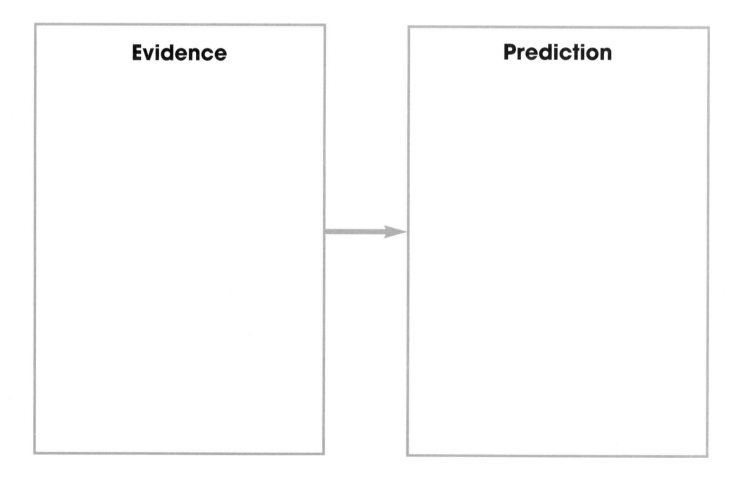

Evidence	**Prediction**

Overview Identifying Sequence of Events in Fiction

Directions and Sample Answers for Activity Pages

Day 1	See "Provide a Real-World Example" below.
Day 2	Read and discuss the story. Then ask students to write signal words from the box to show the sequence of events. (**1:** First. **2:** Next. **3:** As or While. **4:** Before. **5:** while. **6:** After. **7:** As or While. **8:** first.)
Day 3	Read and discuss the story. Then ask students to circle the best answers. (**1:** The Cortas' garage caught on fire. **2:** Mr. Corta told the firefighters that everyone was out. **3:** The firefighters began walking through the garage and house.)
Day 4	Read and discuss the story. Then ask students to record the missing events in the boxes. (**Box 2:** Emma told Mom she and Freckles were going to the park. **Box 5:** Freckles came back out. **Box 6:** Freckles had met a skunk, so Emma said she would give him a bath.)
Day 5	Read the story together. Ask students to record the main events in order on their graphic organizers. Afterward, meet individually with students to discuss their results. Use their responses to plan further instruction and review. (**Box 1:** Mouse accidentally walked on Lion. **Box 2:** Lion was going to eat Mouse. **Box 3:** Lion decided to let Mouse go. **Box 4:** Lion got caught in a trap. **Box 5:** Mouse gnawed the ropes on the trap and set Lion free. **Box 6:** Lion was grateful.)

Provide a Real-World Example

◆ Hand out the Day 1 activity page.

◆ **Say:** *Recently, I e-mailed a friend. I wanted to tell him a funny story, tell him I wouldn't be able to meet him at the library that evening, and tell him about a sale at his favorite store the next day. In what sequence, or order, do you think I wrote these items?* Discuss that you wrote the part about the meeting first. Your friend might not read this important news if he doesn't have time to read the whole e-mail.

◆ Have students locate the underlined word *First*. Explain that *First* is a signal word that helps show the sequence of events. Read the sentence together, and then ask students to put a **1** under the matching picture.

◆ Repeat the process, having students use the signal words *Next* and *Finally* to order the other messages. Allow time for students to share their results and reasons.

◆ Explain that students can also identify a sequence of events when they read stories. Write the following on chart paper:

Identifying Sequence of Events in Fiction

Find clues in the story and pictures.

Find words that tell about order, such as *first, next, as, while, before, after, soon, then,* and *finally.*

Think about the order in which things usually happen.

First Things First

Listen to the example. Then number the pictures in the correct order.

<u>First</u>, I won't be able to meet you at the library tonight.

<u>Next</u>, I want you to know that I found your sunglasses! My cat was wrestling with them!

<u>Finally</u>, I want to tell you there is a sale at your favorite store—everything is 20% off!

Supper Time

Read the story. Then write signal words from the box to show the sequence of events.

After	Before	First	first
While	while	As	Next

  "It's time to make supper!" Mom called. "Everyone on board!"

  (1) _____, Dad began making his famous chili. (2) _____, Ava took the plates from the cupboard and began setting the table. (3) _____ she did this, James baked a cake for dessert and Mom cut up fresh vegetables. (4) _____ they ate, Patty poured dog food into Whiskers's bowl. "You can eat your supper (5) _____ we eat ours," she said as Whiskers wagged his tail.

  (6) _____ supper, Ava took the dirty dishes to the sink. (7) _____ Mom and James washed and dried the dishes, Patty swept the floor around the table, and Dad took the empty cans to the recycling box in the garage.

  "That was a great supper!" said Mom. "Now, how about a movie?"

  "I'm (8) _____ on board!" said Patty as she dashed to the sofa.

Sirens in the Night

Read the story. Then put a check mark beside the best answer to each question.

"r-r-r-R-R-R-R-R-R-R-R-R-r-r-r . . ." blared the sirens. Their shrieks woke Leroy from a deep sleep. Before he opened the blinds on his bedroom window, he smelled smoke. Then, he saw flames across the street.

"The Cortas' garage is on fire!" exclaimed Dad as he ran into the room. Dad opened the window so they could hear what was happening.

"Everyone is safely out of the house!" Mr. Corta called to the firefighters. First, the firefighters connected their hoses. Next, they sprayed the garage. Soon, the fire was out. The firefighters walked through the garage and house to make sure no sparks remained. Before the firefighters left, a Red Cross truck arrived to offer assistance.

Finally, Leroy turned to Dad. "Can we invite the Corta family to stay in our guest room for the rest of the night?" he asked.

"Great idea," said Dad. "I'll go talk to Mr. Corta right now."

1. Which happened first?

The sirens woke Leroy.

Dad ran into Leroy's room.

The Cortas' garage caught on fire.

2. Which happened right after Dad opened the window?

Mr. Corta got everyone safely out of the house.

Mr. Corta told the firefighters that everyone was out.

The firefighters smelled smoke.

3. Which happened right before the Red Cross truck arrived?

The firefighters began walking through the garage and house.

The firefighters sprayed the garage.

Dad went to talk to Mr. Corta.

Emma and Freckles

Read the story. Then write in the empty boxes to show the sequence of events.

"Woof!" barked Freckles. He pulled his leash from the hook by the back door and dropped it in front of Emma.

"I can take a hint!" laughed Emma. "Mom! Freckles and I are going to the park for a few minutes!" she called as she snapped the leash onto her dog's collar.

The park was bordered on two sides by woods. As Freckles sniffed around, Emma looked at the cloud puffs. Suddenly, the leash jerked from her hand, and Freckles ran into the woods. "Freckles!" she called.

Emma had strict orders not to go into the woods, so she waited at the edge, calling and calling. Soon, Freckles came slinking back. "YUCK!" exclaimed Emma. "You met a skunk in there, didn't you?"

Emma grabbed the leash and headed back home. "It's bath time for you," she said to Freckles. "And I hope you've learned your lesson!"

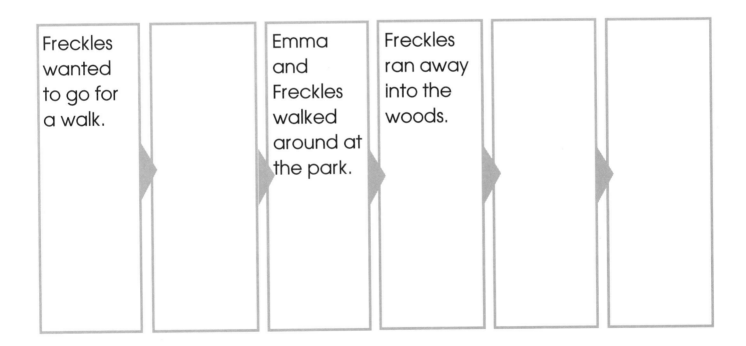

| Freckles wanted to go for a walk. | | Emma and Freckles walked around at the park. | Freckles ran away into the woods. | | |

Assessment

Read the story. Then fill in the boxes with the correct order of the main events.

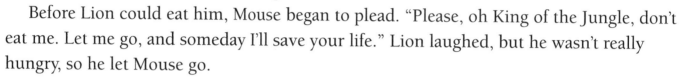

Mouse went for a walk in the jungle. He was daydreaming. The next thing he knew, he walked onto the back of a sleeping lion. "Yikes," he squeaked.

Lion woke up and grabbed Mouse. "What a tasty little treat you'll be," he said, smiling.

Before Lion could eat him, Mouse began to plead. "Please, oh King of the Jungle, don't eat me. Let me go, and someday I'll save your life." Lion laughed, but he wasn't really hungry, so he let Mouse go.

A few days later, Mouse heard someone moaning and found Lion caught in a trap. "Don't worry," Mouse said. "I'll save you." Mouse gnawed and gnawed at the ropes on the trap and finally set Lion free.

"Thank you for keeping your word," said Lion. "I promise to never eat a mouse again."

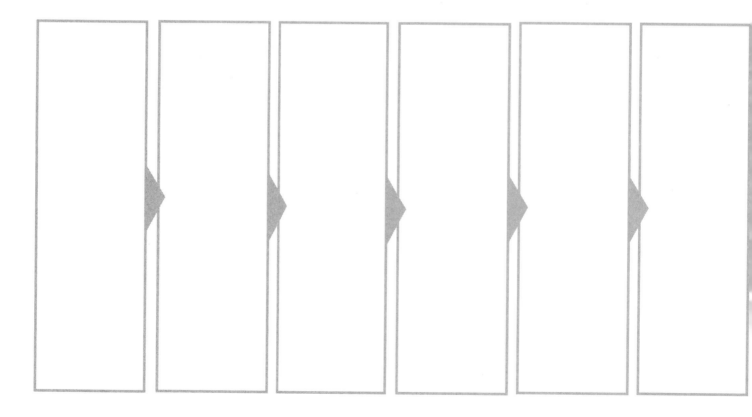

Overview Identifying Sequence of Events in Nonfiction

Directions and Sample Answers for Activity Pages

Day 1	See "Provide a Real-World Example" below.
Day 2	Read and discuss the passage. Then ask students to underline the sequence-of-events signal words and phrases and answer the questions. (**Signal Words and Phrases:** first, after ten years, at this time, soon, several years later, then, today. **1:** He was appointed First Lord of the Admiralty. **2:** He made an unfortunate decision during World War I. **3:** Great Britain declared war on Germany. **4:** He became prime minister of England.)
Day 3	Read and discuss the passage. Then ask students to write signal words from the box to show the correct sequence of the steps. (**1:** In 1859. **2:** Eventually. **3:** First. **4:** Next. **5:** On April 3, 1860. **6:** As. **7:** When. **8:** Finally.)
Day 4	Read and discuss the passage. Then ask students to record the missing events in the boxes. (**Box 2:** Put a dot in the center of the first side. **Box 4:** Draw a line from the top dot to the ends of the side. **Box 6:** Cut out the shape and fold each triangle up along the edge that meets the square.)
Day 5	Read the passage together. Ask students to think about the main events in the development of self-stick notes and record them in order on their graphic organizers. Afterward, meet individually with students to discuss their results. Use their responses to plan further instruction and review. (**Box 1:** A scientist invented a weak adhesive. **Box 2:** A fellow scientist began singing in a choir. **Box 3:** He borrowed his colleague's weak adhesive. **Box 4:** He spread it on the paper strips he used to mark his place in the songbook. **Box 5:** The strips stayed in place, but the scientist could remove them, too. **Box 6:** The scientists' company started selling self-stick notes.)

Provide a Real-World Example

◆ Hand out the Day 1 activity page.

◆ **Say:** *Here are some steps for making a birthday card: Sign your name on the inside. Get some sturdy paper. Write a message on the front and inside. Fold the paper in half. Draw a picture to go with the message. In what sequence, or order, should someone follow these steps?* Discuss that the first step should be to get some sturdy paper, as you cannot make the card without the paper.

◆ Have students locate the word *First* on the left side of the page. Remind students that *First* is a signal word that helps show the correct order of events or steps. Ask students to draw a line from *First* to *Get some sturdy paper.*

◆ Repeat the process with the remaining signal words. Allow time for students to share their reasons for ordering the tasks as they did.

◆ Explain that students can also identify a sequence of events, or steps in a process, when they read. Write the following on chart paper:

Identifying Sequence of Events in Nonfiction

Find evidence in the story and pictures.

Find words that tell about order, such as *eventually, first, next, after that, then, after, soon, today,* and *finally.*

Think about the order in which things usually happen.

Making a Birthday Card

Listen to the steps. Then draw a line from each signal word to the matching step.

First

Sign your name on the inside.

After that

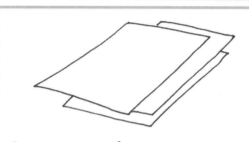

Get some sturdy paper.

Next

Write a message on the front and inside.

Then

Draw a picture to go with the message.

Finally

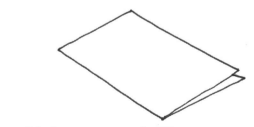

Fold the paper in half.

Winston Churchill

Read the passage. Underline the sequence-of-events signal words and phrases. Then answer the questions.

Born in England, Winston Churchill loved his country. He wanted to serve in its government and sought a career in politics. His first political role began in 1901 when he entered Parliament, Great Britain's government. After ten years, he was appointed First Lord of the Admiralty. Churchill's political career was successful at this time. Soon, however, he became the head of the Royal Navy, made an unfortunate decision during World War I, and had to resign. Several years later, Churchill warned the government again and again of Adolf Hitler's plan to invade England. Hitler did indeed approach England, and Great Britain declared war on Germany. Then, on September 4, 1939, Winston Churchill became prime minister of his country. Today, many people around the world remember Winston Churchill as a great leader and respected statesman.

1. What role did Churchill have ten years after he entered Parliament?

_____

2. What happened before Churchill had to resign as head of the Royal Navy?

_____

3. What happened after Hitler approached England?

_____

4. What was Churchill's next political role?

_____

The Pony Express

Read the passage. Then write signal words from the box to show the sequence of events.

When	Eventually
On April 13, 1860	As
In 1859	Finally
First	Next

(1) _____, mail delivery from the eastern part of the United States to California was very slow. (2) _____, three men had an idea for a speedier way to deliver mail and founded the Pony Express. (3) _____, they built relay stations about 10 to 15 miles (about 16 to 24 kilometers) apart. (4) _____, they purchased horses and hired expert riders. (5) _____, the first rider climbed on his horse in St. Joseph, Missouri, and headed west with saddlebags full of mail. (6) _____ he traveled, he stopped at the relay stations to change horses. (7) _____ he got to a station where another rider waited, that rider put the saddlebags on a fresh horse and took over. (8) _____, the last rider arrived in Sacramento, California—nearly 2,000 miles (about 3,200 kilometers) away!

   Unit 4 • Everyday Comprehension Intervention Activities Grade 5 • ©2010 Newmark Learning, LLC

Paper Pyramid

Read the passage. Then write in the empty boxes to show the sequence of events.

A pyramid is a solid shape. The bottom is a square, and the four sides are triangles. The triangles meet at the top, forming a point. You can make a pyramid out of paper. First, draw a square. Each side should be four inches long. Then, put a dot in the center of the first side. Put another dot four inches above the dot. This dot will be the point of your first triangle. Next, draw a line from the top dot to the ends of the side. That way, your triangle will be the correct size to form a pyramid. Repeat the process with the other three sides of the square. When you are done, cut out the shape. Fold each triangle up along the edge that meets the square. Finally, tape the sides together.

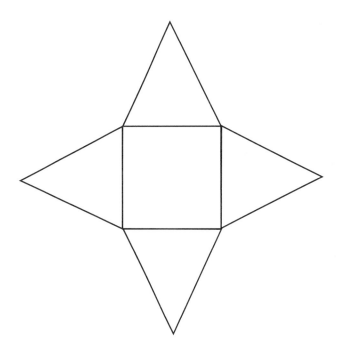

Draw a square with four-inch sides.		Put a dot four inches above the first dot.		Repeat the process with the other three sides of the square.		Tape the sides together.

Assessment

Read the passage. Then fill in the boxes to show the correct order of events.

Self-stick notes are a popular product. They stick to paper but peel off without damaging either the paper or the note. Did you know that self-stick notes were the result of a failed invention? First, a scientist invented a new adhesive. However, the adhesive was too weak. It would stick to things, but he could easily remove it. Soon, he stopped working on his invention. Several years later, a fellow scientist was singing in a choir. The paper strips he used to mark his place in the songbook kept falling out. He borrowed his colleague's weak adhesive. Then, he spread the adhesive on his paper strips. Finally, the strips stayed in place, yet he could take them off without harming the songbook. Not long after that, the scientists' company started selling self-stick notes as a new product.

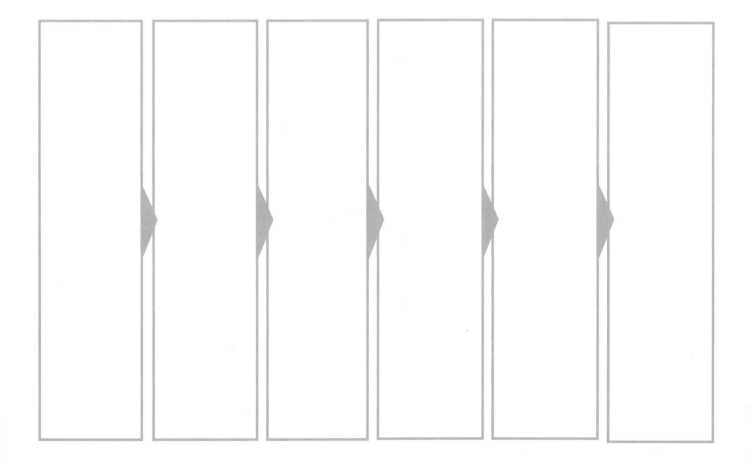

Overview Analyzing Story Elements: Setting

Directions and Sample Answers for Activity Pages

Day 1	See "Provide a Real-World Example" below.
Day 2	Read and discuss the story. Then ask students to answer the questions. (**1:** at a county fair. **2:** goat barn, show ring, biggest pumpkin in the county, horse barn, old-time cars, country band, Spinning Wheel, draft horses, blue ribbon, ice cream cones. **3:** summer. **4:** outdoor activities, ice cream cones.)
Day 3	Read and discuss the story and setting clues. Then ask students to circle the best answers. (**1:** on a plane. **Clues:** smiling woman in the doorway; special seat right here in front; end of the flight; fastened her seat belt. **2:** in the present day. **Clues:** backpack, CD.)
Day 4	Read and discuss the story. Then ask students to complete the sentence and color the circle in front of each setting clue from the story. (the Winter Olympics. **Clues:** ski jumping, opening ceremony, parka, competition, around the world, torch, gold medal, tickets.)
Day 5	Read the story together. Ask students to use clues in the story to figure out the setting and record their ideas on their graphic organizers. Afterward, meet individually with students to discuss their results. Use their responses to plan further instruction and review. (**Clues:** steps, books, new contraption, office, typewriter, walk to a store to call a friend, maybe someone will invent a phone you can carry in your car. **Setting:** in front of a school in the days before computers and cell phones were invented.)

Provide a Real-World Example

◆ Hand out the Day 1 activity page.

◆ **Say:** *Certain activities happen at certain places and times. For example, we have class at this school building on weekdays. Some kids play soccer at the park on Saturday mornings. My friend's dog sleeps on a pillow at the foot of her bed at night. Some of your parents might buy groceries at the store on their way home from work. Where and when something takes place is called a setting.*

◆ **Say:** Ask students to list activities in the left column of the T-chart and a setting for each activity in the right column. Remind them that setting includes both place and time. Then invite students to share their ideas with the group.

◆ Explain that they can also analyze settings when they read stories. Write the following on chart paper:

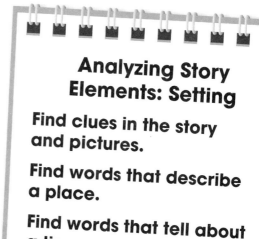

Analyzing Story Elements: Setting

Find clues in the story and pictures.

Find words that describe a place.

Find words that tell about a time.

Think about when and where an event could happen.

Where and When

Brainstorm a list of activities. Then list the setting for each activity.

Activity	Setting

Gruff's Blue Ribbon

Read the story. Then answer the questions.

Robert and Ethan wandered into the goat barn, looking for Jen. They found her in the end stall with Gruff. She was brushing Gruff's long, silky hair. "He looks great, Jen," Robert said. "When do you take him in the show ring?"

"In about 20 minutes," Jen answered.

"OK, we'll come back then," Ethan said. "Hey, Robert, let's go see who won the pumpkin contest."

After the boys admired the biggest pumpkin in the county, they headed for the horse barn, passing old-time cars on the way. A country band was playing, and kids on the Spinning Wheel were screaming. "Whoa! Look at those draft horses!" Robert exclaimed. "They're huge!"

Robert and Ethan got back to the show ring in time to see Gruff win a blue ribbon. "Way to go!" the boys yelled. They helped Jen get Gruff settled in his stall.

"How about some ice cream cones now?" asked Jen.

1. Where does the story take place? _____

2. What clues did you use to answer question 1? _____

_____

3. When does the story take place? _____

4. What clues did you use to answer question 3? _____

_____

Karina's Surprise

Read the story. Draw a line under the setting clues.
Then draw a circle around the best answer to each question.

"Hello!" said the smiling woman in the doorway. "We have a special seat for you right here in front. I promised your mom I'd take care of you until your dad picks you up at the end of the flight."

"Thank you!" said Karina. She pulled a book out of her backpack, pushed the backpack under the seat, and fastened her seatbelt.

"Hi!" said a pleasant voice as someone buckled in beside her.

Karina looked up. Then, her eyes flew wide open. "You're . . . you're . . ." she stammered.

"Yes, I am," said the young woman with a grin. "And here's a copy of my latest CD to prove it!"

"Wow," said Karina, closing her book. "This is going to be the best flight ever!"

1. Where does the story take place?

   on a train

   at an airport

   on a plane

2. When does the story take place?

   long ago

   in the present day

   in the future

Ski Jumping

Read the story. Complete the sentence. Then color the circle in front of each setting clue from the story.

"I can't believe we're really here!" Sam exclaimed. He and Dad watched as skiers from around the world gathered at their competition area.

"I can't believe I actually got tickets . . . and time off from work," Dad laughed. "What has been your favorite part so far?"

"I loved seeing the runner with the torch arrive at the opening ceremonies," said Sam, pulling up the hood of his parka. The temperature had dropped, but no way was he going inside to warm up. "I think my favorite part is coming up now, though—ski jumping! I can't wait to see who wins the gold medal!"

This story takes place at _____.

Setting Clues

○ Sam

○ ski jumping

○ opening ceremony

○ favorite part

○ parka

○ competition

○ Dad

○ around the world

○ time off from work

○ torch

○ gold medal

○ tickets

Assessment

Read the story. Then fill in the boxes to show the setting.

Dane and Marta sat on the steps. "I wonder where Dad is," said Dane.

"I know—he's never late," said Marta. She put her books on the ground. "Hey, did you see the new contraption in Miss Winter's office? It's called a typewriter!"

"Yes!" said Dane. "She showed me how it works, too. You put paper in it, and then you hit the keys, and then letters appear on the paper. She said it's faster than writing things out by hand—easier to read, too."

"Just imagine—we might have our own typewriter someday," dreamed Marta.

Suddenly, Dad pulled up. "Sorry, kids," he said. "I had a flat tire, and my jack wasn't in the trunk. I had to walk to a store to call a friend for help."

"That's okay, Dad," said Dane. "Who knows, maybe someday someone will invent a phone you can carry in your car!"

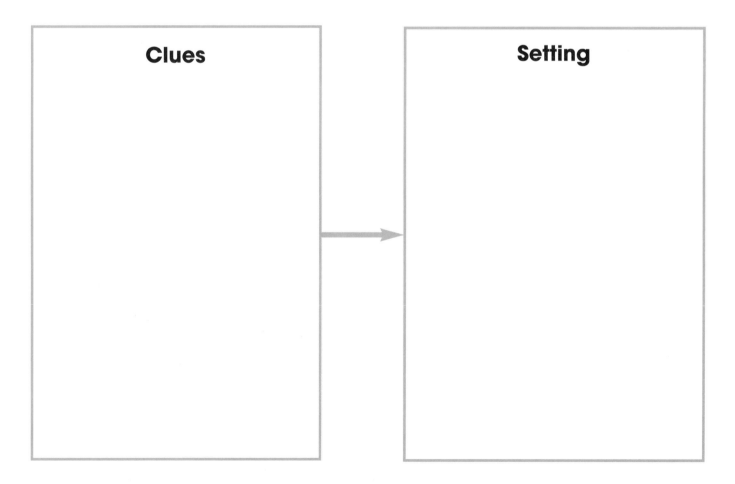

Clues	Setting

Overview Analyzing Story Elements: Plot

Directions and Sample Answers for Activity Pages

Day 1	See "Provide a Real-World Example" below.
Day 2	Read and discuss the story. Then ask students to circle the best answers. (**1:** Shyann makes fun of Sabrina in gym class. **2:** Shyann was jealous of Sabrina's math score. **3:** Sabrina practices jumping rope so she can get better, and then she shows Shyann that they are still friends.)
Day 3	Read and discuss the story. Then ask students to circle the best answers. (**1:** Mario and Kevin **2:** Mario and Kevin need a way to talk to each other on a regular basis. **3:** Mario will e-mail Kevin from his grandparents' computer or the city library.)
Day 4	Read and discuss the myth. Then ask students to answer the questions. (**1:** King Minos forced his people to sacrifice youths and maidens to a Minotaur. **2:** Theseus volunteers to be one of the youths to go inside the maze, where he will find and fight the Minotaur. **3:** Theseus might get lost in the maze. Ariadne gives him a magic ball of string to help him find his way. **4:** He defeats the Minotaur.)
Day 5	Read the story together. Ask students to record the problem and solution on their graphic organizers. Afterward, meet individually with students to discuss their results. Use their responses to plan further instruction and review. (**Problem:** Brin can't carry two bags of apples on her bike. **Solution:** She will take the first bag home, and then she will return for the second bag.)

Provide a Real-World Example

◆ Hand out the Day 1 activity page.

◆ **Say:** *A group of students wanted to form a chess club at their school. What problems might they encounter? How could the students work to solve these problems?*

◆ Discuss that a school club must be approved by the principal. One solution could be to make a list of all the ways a chess club would benefit the school, schedule a meeting to share the list with the principal, and then ask for permission to start a club.

◆ Invite student partners to brainstorm other problems and solutions and write their ideas on the lines. If students are stuck, ask questions such as *Who will sponsor the club? Where will the club meet? When will the club meet? Where will the club get chess boards and pieces to use at school?*

◆ Remind students that these situations are like the plot of a story. **Say:** *A story has one or more problems and solutions to make it interesting to read.* Write the following on chart paper:

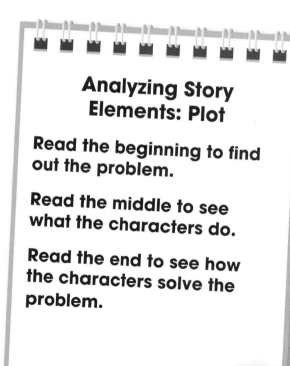

Analyzing Story Elements: Plot

Read the beginning to find out the problem.

Read the middle to see what the characters do.

Read the end to see how the characters solve the problem.

Chess Club

Listen to the example. Write the problem and solution. Then brainstorm other possible problems and solutions.

Problem: _____

Solution: _____

Problem: _____

Solution: _____

Problem: _____

Solution: _____

Problem: _____

Solution: _____

Gym Class

Read the story. Then draw a circle around the best answer to each question.

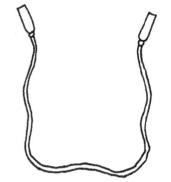

"Shyann made fun of me in gym today," Sabrina complained at dinner. "I'm not very good at jumping rope."

"Why don't you tell the teacher?" asked her little brother Marcus.

"I don't want to be a whiner," Sabrina replied.

"I'll help you practice after dinner," said her big sister Emily. "I'll ask Cora to come over, too. She's REALLY good!"

Sabrina, Emily, and Cora practiced every night that week. "I can't wait until gym class on Monday," said Sabrina.

On Monday morning, Sabrina took her place beside Shyann. "Wow!" said Shyann. "How did you get so good?"

"I practiced," said Sabrina.

"I'm sorry I teased you," said Shyann. "I was just jealous because you got a better math score than I did. Will you show me how to do some of those fancy jumps?"

"Sure!" said Sabrina. "You can come to my house after school. And maybe we can do our math homework together, too!"

1. What is the problem in the story?

Sabrina is better at math than Shyann is.

Shyann makes fun of Sabrina in gym class.

Shyann is better at jumping rope than Sabrina is.

2. What is the true cause of the problem?

Shyann was jealous of Sabrina's math score.

Sabrina made fun of Shyann about her math score.

Sabrina was jealous of Shyann's jump-rope skills.

3. What is the solution to the problem?

Sabrina tells on Shyann, and the teacher helps them work things out.

Shyann says she will be friends again if Sabrina will help her with her math homework.

Sabrina practices jumping rope so she can get better, and then she shows Shyann that they are still friends.

Moving to Mexico

Read the story. Then circle the best answer to each question.

"I just found out that we're moving to Mexico," Mario told Kevin. "I'm excited to live near my grandparents again. But you're my best friend. We see each other every day. Who will I talk to about school? And movies? And our favorite sports teams?"

"Maybe we can call each other on weekends," replied Kevin.

"I think phone calls would be too expensive," said Mario.

"We could write letters," Kevin suggested.

"Letters take too long to go back and forth," Mario said sadly. "I wish I had a computer so we could e-mail."

Mario's sister walked by. "Our *abuelo* and *abuela* have a computer," she said. "They e-mail Mom at work all the time. Or you could go to the city library and use the computers there."

"Yeah!" said Kevin. "Next time you're at my house, I'll help you set up an e-mail address so you can write me the minute you get to Mexico!"

1. Who has a problem?

Mario

Kevin

Mario and Kevin

Mario's sister

2. What is the problem?

Mario's family needs to buy a computer.

Kevin needs to write letters to Mario more often.

Mario needs more money so he can call Kevin on weekends.

Mario and Kevin need a way to talk to each other on a regular basis.

3. What is the characters' solution to the problem?

Kevin will e-mail Mario from his grandparents' computer or the city library.

Mario will e-mail Kevin from his grandparents' computer or the city library.

Both boys will use their grandparents' computers to e-mail each other.

Both boys will go to the city library to e-mail each other.

The Minotaur

Read the myth. Then read the questions and write your answers.

Long ago, King Minos of Crete had a Minotaur—a terrible monster that was half man and half bull. The king kept the Minotaur in a maze. Every year, the king forced his people to sacrifice seven youths and seven maidens to the Minotaur.

Then, a young man named Theseus came along. "Choose me to go into the maze," Theseus said. "Then I will find the Minotaur and fight him to the end."

Before Theseus entered, the king's beautiful daughter Ariadne slipped out of the palace and gave him a magic ball of string. "The maze is tricky, my brave Theseus," she said. "You might get lost. This ball of string will unwind to show you where to find the Minotaur, and then it will lead you out."

Theseus defeated the Minotaur and escaped the maze. He then left with Ariadne at his side. But . . . that's another story!

1. Reread the beginning of the myth. What is the problem?

_____

_____

2. Reread the middle of the myth. How does Theseus decide to solve the problem?

_____

_____

3. What obstacle might Theseus meet as he tries to solve the problem? How does Ariadne help him overcome this obstacle?

_____

_____

4. Reread the end of the myth. How does Theseus solve the people's problem?

_____

_____

Assessment

Read the story. Then fill in the boxes with the problem and solution.

Brin was riding her bike to the orchard to buy Mom a bag of apples when she saw a sign: *Buy one bag of apples. Get the second bag free.* "What a bargain!" she said. Then her face fell. How would she get two bags home? The basket on her bike would only hold one.

Brin thought for a moment. She could ask to borrow the farmer's cell phone and call Mom to come help her, but Mom was busy. She could try to balance the second bag on her lap, but it was heavy and she might fall. "I know!" she said. She put the first bag in her basket. "Will you put my other bag under the table?" she asked the farmer. "I'll be right back for it!"

Mom was happy to let Brin make a return trip to the orchard. And Brin was happy to eat homemade apple pie for dinner that night!

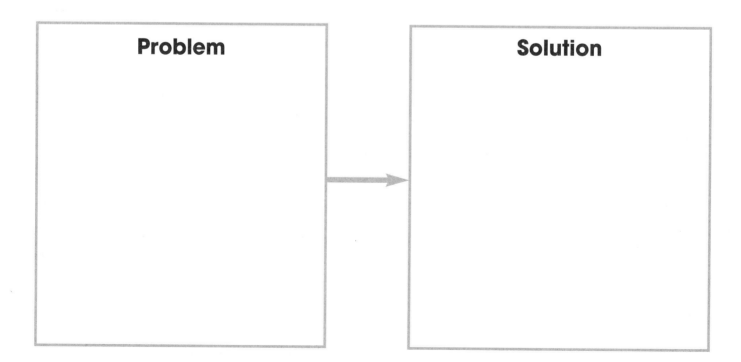

Problem	**Solution**

Overview Analyzing Character: Traits and Feelings

Directions and Sample Answers for Activity Pages

Day 1	See "Provide a Real-World Example" below.
Day 2	Read and discuss the story. Then ask students to answer the questions. (Answers will vary, but could include **1:** Crow is an eager learner. He comes to the woods every day. **2:** Crow is curious. He wants to hear the stories. **3:** The stone is wise. It knows about the world and all its creatures. **4:** The stone is grateful. It has found someone who will pass the stories on.)
Day 3	Read and discuss the story. Then ask students to circle the words that best describe the characters' traits and feelings. (**1:** bothered. **2:** creative. **3:** surprised. **4:** wise.)
Day 4	Read and discuss the story. Then ask students to circle the best answers. (**1:** Rodrigo is loving. **2:** Dad felt a sense of urgency. **3:** Rodrigo told Dad to hurry. **4:** The lifeguard is conscientious. **5:** Dad is modest.)
Day 5	Read the story together. Ask students to write about Alma's traits and feelings on their graphic organizers. Afterward, meet individually with students to discuss their results. Use their responses to plan further instruction and review. (**Clues/Traits:** slouched down in seat; didn't want teacher to call on her; didn't want classmates to stare at her/shy. **Clues/Traits:** read the chapter; went online to find out more; discussed topic with family at dinner; often helped classmates with social studies homework/studious, intelligent. **Clues/Feelings:** mouth went dry; cheeks turned red/anxious, nervous. **Clues/Feelings:** smiled and sat up straighter/relieved.)

Provide a Real-World Example

◆ Hand out the Day 1 activity page.

◆ **Say:** *I recently read about a girl who lost her wallet. The next day, a boy brought the wallet to her door. He had found it on the sidewalk and looked up her address in the phone book. Nothing was missing from the wallet.*

◆ Write the words *traits* and *feelings* on the board. **Say:** *A trait is a special quality about a person. It is the way a person usually is. I can think of some traits that describe the boy. The boy is considerate and trustworthy.* Allow time for students to write these traits beside the picture of the boy and share others they think apply. Then **say:** *A feeling is something that changes with the situation. What feelings do you think the girl experienced?* Allow time for students to share their ideas and write them on the page.

◆ Explain that students can also analyze a character's traits and feelings when they read stories. Write the following on chart paper:

Analyzing Character: Traits and Feelings

Find clues in the pictures and words.

Think about what a character thinks, says, and does.

Think of words that describe the character.

Think of words that describe how the character feels.

The Missing Wallet

Listen to the story. Then list the traits of the boy and the feelings of the girl.

Traits

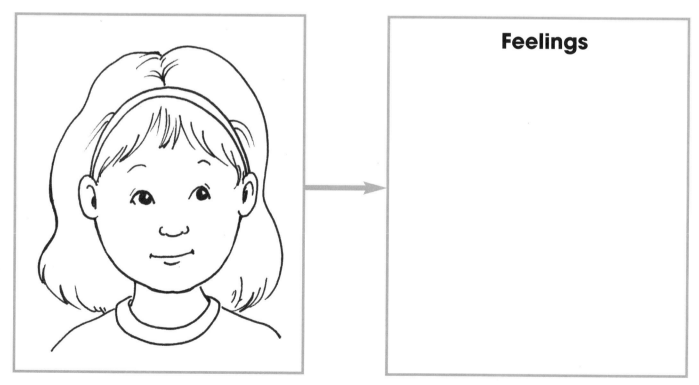

Feelings

The Storytelling Stone

Read the story. Then answer each question.

Long ago, a boy named Crow went into the woods to hunt. After a few hours, he spotted a flat, smooth stone. "I'll sit here to rest," he said.

Suddenly, he heard a raspy voice. "Let me tell you a story," said the voice. Startled, Crow jumped up from the stone and looked around. "Let me tell you a story," the voice said again. This time, Crow realized that the voice came from the stone.

"I don't know what a story is," said Crow.

"Listen and learn," said the stone.

Every day after that, Crow came to the woods to hear stories about the world and all its creatures. One day, the stone said, "Now you must share the stories with others. You will be the first storyteller. Tell everyone they must pass the stories on until the end of time." And Crow did.

1. What is Crow like? How do you know?

_____

2. How does Crow feel? How do you know?

_____

3. What is the stone like? How do you know?

_____

4. How does the stone feel? How do you know?

_____

A Lesson Learned

Read the story. Then draw a circle around the word that belongs in each blank.

Young Ben Franklin was catching minnows around the edge of a pond with his friends. "My feet are getting wet," his pal complained.

"I know where we can get some stepping stones," said Ben.

Ben and his friends walked to a nearby area where workers were building a house. "Look at all those building stones!" whispered Ben. "Let's wait until the workers are done for the day. Then we'll take a few—they won't miss them."

The next morning, the workers looked around. "Hey—where are the rest of the stones?" they asked. They immediately set out on a search. Soon, they found Ben and his friends using the stones in the pond.

All the boys got in trouble. "But we needed those stones," Ben argued.

Ben's father disagreed. "Nothing is useful which is not honest," he said. Ben remembered that lesson for the rest of his life.

1. At the beginning of the story, Ben's pal felt _____.

      pleased   bothered   embarrassed

2. Ben's friends thought he was being _____.

      creative   cranky   bossy

3. The workers felt _____ when they got to the new house the next morning.

      frightened   relieved   surprised

4. Ben's father was _____ to handle Ben's crime in the way he did.

      brave   wise   rude

Rescue!

Read the story. Then draw a circle around the best answer to each question.

"I love the beach!" Rodrigo told Dad. "I wish mom and Maddie could have come with us."

Suddenly, a woman nearby screamed. "My daughter! She's out too far! She can't fight the current!"

Before the lifeguard could climb down from his stand, Rodrigo's dad was swimming out to the girl. As he swam, Rodrigo saw the girl go under once, twice, and then a third time. "Hurry, Dad!" he called.

A moment later, Dad lifted the girl's head out of the water. She sputtered, then took a deep breath. "I've got you now," Dad said soothingly. "Let's get back to your mom."

The lifeguard met them halfway and helped bring the girl in. An EMT was already waiting.

"You're a hero!" exclaimed Rodrigo.

"No, I'm just doing what any good swimmer would have done," said Dad.

1. Rodrigo wished his mom and sister could have come to the beach with them. What trait does this suggest?

    Rodrigo is cooperative.   Rodrigo is loving.

2. The woman was screaming. How did this make Dad feel?

    Dad felt a sense of urgency.   Dad felt agitated.

3. Think about how Rodrigo felt as he watched Dad swim out to the girl. What clue is in the story?

    Rodrigo told Dad to hurry.   Rodrigo watched the lifeguard
                                            climb down from his stand.

4. The lifeguard had already called for an EMT. What trait does this suggest?

    The lifeguard is impatient.   The lifeguard is conscientious.

5. Think about what Dad said when Rodrigo called him a hero. What trait does this suggest?

    Dad is conceited.   Dad is modest.

Assessment

Read the story. Then fill in the boxes to show at least one trait and one feeling.

"Maybe if I slouch down in my seat, the teacher won't call on me," thought Alma. It wasn't that she hadn't done her social studies homework—quite the opposite. She had read the chapter and knew all about the transcontinental railroad. Since she had some questions the book didn't answer, she had gone online to find out even more. Then, she discussed the railroad with her family at dinner and found out that one of her long-ago relatives had helped build it! She often helped her classmates with their social studies homework, but somehow she couldn't answer a question when everyone was staring at her.

Alma saw the teacher looking over the class. Her mouth went dry, and her cheeks turned red. "Paul, please share your homework answers today," said the teacher. Alma smiled and sat up straighter. Maybe class was going to be okay after all!

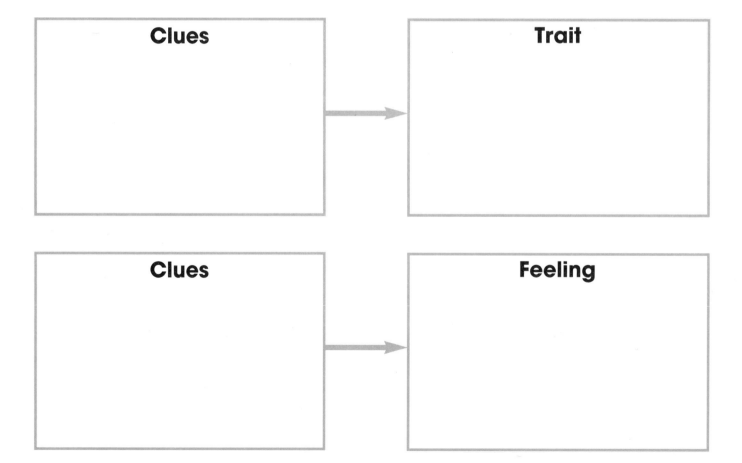

Clues	**Trait**

Clues	**Feeling**

Overview Analyzing Character: Relationships and Changes

Directions and Sample Answers for Activity Pages

Day 1	See "Provide a Real-World Example" below.
Day 2	Read and discuss the story. Then ask students to circle the best answers. (**1:** friends. **2:** complimentary. **3:** friendly to stubborn. **4:** reasonable, fair. **5:** "Yes!")
Day 3	Read and discuss the story. Then ask students to circle the words that belong in the blanks. (**1:** upset. **2:** brothers. **3:** impatient. **4:** considerate. **5:** excited. **6:** relieved.)
Day 4	Read and discuss the story. Then ask students to color the circle in front of each true statement. (Mona is Domino's older sister. Mona and Domino are going on vacation with their dad. Mona and Domino can both be stubborn at times. At first, Mona and Domino only thought about themselves. At the end of the story, Mona and Domino worked out a fair plan.)
Day 5	Read the story together. Ask students to write about Marta's relationships and changes on their graphic organizers. Afterward, meet individually with students to discuss their results. Use their responses to plan further instruction and review. (**Clues/Relationship:** heard the power saw and hammer, knocked on the door, Marta knew Mrs. Knipp/neighbors **Clues/Change:** complained about noise, brought over a carrot cake/from irritated to thoughtful.)

Provide a Real-World Example

◆ Hand out the Day 1 activity page.

◆ **Say:** *I know two girls who used to walk to school together. Then, I noticed that they started coming separately. They quit chatting with each other at school, too.*

◆ Write the words **relationships** and **changes** on the board. **Say:** *People have many types of relationships. They can be family members, friends, or neighbors. I think the girls I mentioned are neighbors, since they walked to school together.* Allow time for students to write about this relationship in the box. Then **say:** *People sometimes change as time goes on. They change in many ways and for many reasons. At first, the girls I mentioned seemed like friends. How did that relationship change?* Allow time for students to share their ideas and write them on the page.

◆ Repeat the process for the second set of pictures. Then explain that students can also analyze characters' relationships and changes when they read stories. Write the following on chart paper:

Analyzing Character: Relationships and Changes

Use clues in the pictures and words to figure out . . .

• which characters are in the same family

• which characters are friends or neighbors

• which characters go to the same school or job

• how the characters think, feel, and act at the beginning of the story

• how they think, feel, and act at the end of the story

• what makes them change

Friends?

Listen to the example. Then write your ideas in the boxes.

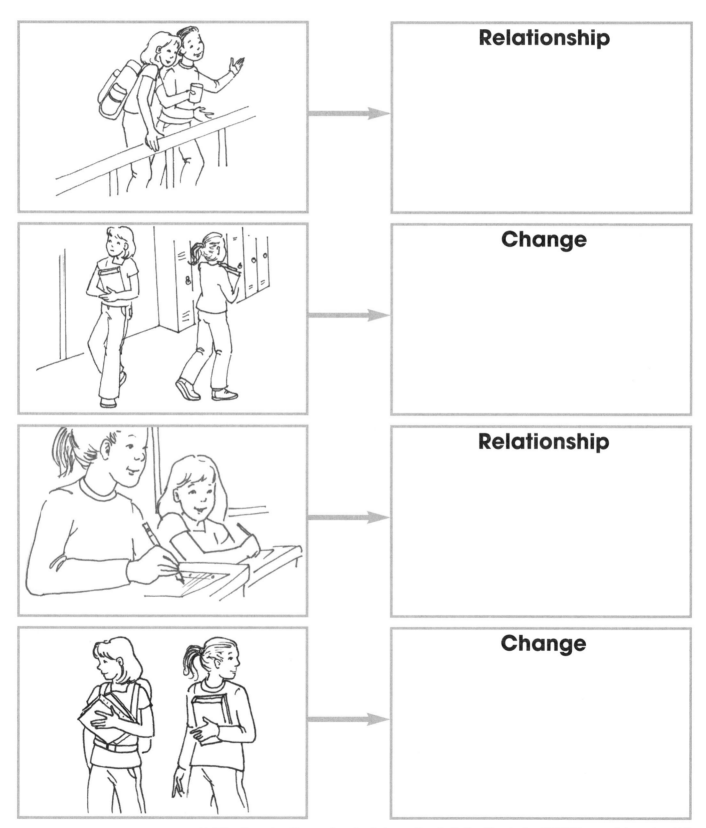

The Arctics

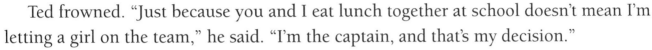

**Read the story. Then draw a circle around
the best answer for each question.**

"How did you get to be such a great ice hockey player?"
asked Ted as he glided across the ice.

"I've been playing with my brothers since I was little,"
Sara replied. "Now I want to join the Arctics. You're on a
losing streak right now, and I could be a big help."

Ted frowned. "Just because you and I eat lunch together at school doesn't mean I'm
letting a girl on the team," he said. "I'm the captain, and that's my decision."

Sara shrugged her shoulders. "Think about it," she said.

Sara kept practicing every day. Ted avoided her, but she smiled and waved when she
saw him across the lunchroom. Soon, she got the e-mail she was waiting for.

The guys and I have reconsidered. Will you play in our game this Saturday? Ted
Sara hit Reply.
Yes! See you at practice tonight. Sara

1. What is the relationship between Ted and Sara?	brother and sister	friends
2. What is Ted like at the beginning of the story?	complimentary	indifferent
3. How does Ted change in the middle of the story?	friendly to stubborn	curious to greedy
4. What traits does Ted show at the end of the story?	skeptical, glum	reasonable, fair
5. Which is a clue to how Sara feels after Ted's e-mail?	Sara hit Reply.	"Yes!"

The Library

**Read the story. Then draw a circle around
the word that belongs in each blank.**

"I don't want to go to the library," Quentin whined.
"It's boring."

"Mom says I have to take you with me," said Greg.
"Now, quit acting like a baby."

When the boys got to the library, Greg found a chair by the checkout desk. "Stay
here," he commanded. Quentin frowned and crossed his arms over his chest. But soon, he
heard laughter from a nearby room.

"We're having a puppet show," a woman said. "After that, we'll have a story, crafts, and
a snack. Come join us!"

A few minutes later, Greg came to look for Quentin. He was gone! Panic set in. "Have
you seen a little boy?" he asked the librarian at the desk. "He was sitting right here."

The woman smiled. "He's probably in with the other children," she said. When Greg
opened the door, Quentin spotted him and came over. "I don't want to leave yet,"
Quentin whispered. "The library is fun!"

1. At the beginning of the story, Quentin was ____.   upset   mischievous

2. Quentin and Greg were probably ____.   neighbors   brothers

3. Greg was ____ with Quentin.   impatient   reasonable

**4. The ____ woman invited Quentin to join the
  other children.**   considerate   tolerant

5. At the end of the story, Quentin was ____.   inquisitive   excited

6. When Greg found Quentin, Greg probably felt ____.   relieved   annoyed

Off to Colorado

Read the story. Then color the circle in front of every statement that is true.

"Time to go. Colorado, here we come!" Dad called.

Mona and Domino ran out of the house with their backpacks. "I'm sitting in the front seat," Mona said.

"I want to sit in the front seat. I'm smaller," said Domino.

"Too bad," said Mona. "I want to get a good view of the bighorn sheep."

"Me, too," Domino replied. "I brought my camera, and it's hard to get good pictures from the back."

"Come on, kids," said Dad. "We need to hit the road."

Mona thought a moment. "Let's take turns," she suggested. "You can go first. Then, every time we stop for a break, we can switch."

"Okay!" said Domino. "And if I get some good pictures while you're in the back, I'll print copies for you!"

○ Domino is Mona's older brother.

○ Mona is Domino's older sister.

○ Mona and Domino are going on vacation with their dad.

○ Mona, Domino, and Dad live in Colorado.

○ Mona and Domino can both be stubborn at times.

○ At first, Mona was considerate and Domino was selfish.

○ At first, Mona and Domino only thought about themselves.

○ Dad helped Mona and Domino solve their problem.

○ At the end of the story, Domino suggested a compromise.

○ At the end of the story, Mona and Domino worked out a fair plan.

Assessment

**Read the story. Then fill in the boxes to show
one relationship and one change.**

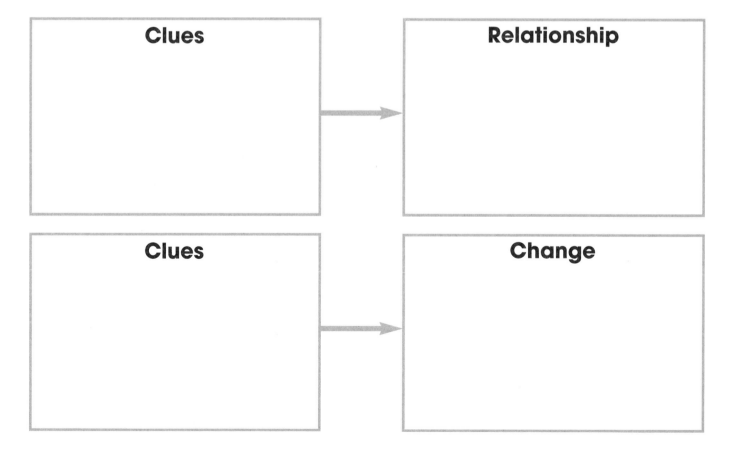

Mrs. Knipp knocked on the door. "Hi," she said. "I heard the power saw screeching at six this morning . . . not a very pleasant way to wake up!"

Marta blushed. "I'm sorry, Mrs. Knipp. We're building a little deck out back. Dad and Mom will be finished sawing in just a bit."

Two hours later, Mrs. Knipp knocked again. "All that hammering is giving me a headache," she said.

"I'm so sorry," said Marta. "They'll be done hammering in about an hour."

"Then I'll go to the store," said Mrs. Knipp. "At least it'll be quieter there."

Later that day, Mrs. Knipp knocked on the door a third time. "Hi!" said Marta. "What's wrong?"

"Nothing," said Mrs. Knipp. "I just brought over some carrot cake."

Marta smiled. "And Dad just made tea! Please join us for a snack on our new deck!"

Clues	Relationship

Clues	Change

Overview Identifying Stated Main Idea and Supporting Details

Directions and Sample Answers for Activity Pages

Day 1	See "Provide a Real-World Example" below.
Day 2	Read and discuss the paragraph. Then ask students to draw a circle around the best answers. (**1:** The classification of animals known as marsupials is made up of mostly "pouched" animals. **2:** A bandicoot can be as large as a rabbit. **3:** A Tasmanian devil preys on animals larger than itself. A wombat is shy.)
Day 3	Read and discuss the paragraph. Then ask students to underline the stated main idea and draw a line from the name of each piece of equipment to its supporting detail. (**Stated Main Idea:** In order to snorkel, a swimmer needs a few pieces of simple equipment. **Wetsuit:** to stay warm. **Swim fins:** to swim faster. **Snorkel:** to breathe. **Snorkeling vest:** to float. **Snorkeling mask:** to protect eyes.)
Day 4	Read and discuss the paragraph. Then ask students to write the stated main idea and supporting details. (**Stated Main Idea:** Butterflies have several ways to protect themselves from predators. **Monarch:** poisonous. **Viceroy:** looks like a monarch. **Indian leaf:** looks like a dead leaf. **Buckeye:** has spots on its wings that look like large eyes.)
Day 5	Read the paragraph together. Ask students to record the stated main idea and supporting details. Afterward, meet individually with students to discuss their results. Use their responses to plan further instruction and review. (**Stated Main Idea:** Lightning can be dangerous. **Supporting Details:** swimming pools close; sports events are cancelled; second leading cause of storm deaths in the United States; seriously injures many others; National Weather Service has safety rules.)

Provide a Real-World Example

◆ Hand out the Day 1 activity page.

◆ **Say:** *Many people like to take photographs. Some people have cameras with film. Other people use digital cameras. Still other people take pictures with their cell phones.* Ask students to complete the main idea you stated. Then ask them to circle the details you added. **Say:** *Mentioning these different types of cameras supports the idea that people like to take photographs.*

◆ Ask students to read the second stated main idea. Then invite them to list details that support the main idea, such as *in photo albums, on their computers, in scrapbooks, in their wallets, on social networking Web sites,* and *displayed in picture frames.*

◆ Explain that students can also find stated main ideas and supporting details when they read. **Say:** *The main idea is the most important statement. The supporting details tell more about the main idea.* Then write the following on chart paper:

Identifying Stated Main Idea and Supporting Details

See what the paragraph is about.

Find the sentence that states the most important idea.

Find details that support, or give more information about, the main idea.

Photographs

Listen to the example. Complete the stated main idea. Then discuss the supporting details.

Stated Main Idea: Many people like to _____.

Read the following statement. Then list supporting details.

Stated Main Idea: People store and display their photographs in different places.

_____

_____

_____

_____

_____

Marsupials

**Read the paragraph. Then draw a circle around the best
answer to each question.**

Most people know that kangaroos have pockets. Did
you know that some other animals have pockets, too? The
classification of animals known as marsupials is made up
of mostly "pouched" animals. One of the most common
marsupials is the opossum, which looks more like a large rat than a kangaroo. Another
marsupial is the bandicoot, which can be as large as a rabbit. Bandicoots can hop on their
back legs like a kangaroo or creep on all fours. A Tasmanian devil is a fierce-looking
marsupial that preys on animals larger than itself. A wombat is a shy marsupial that can
dig a burrow 100 feet long. Another marsupial looks like a koala—because it is a koala!
Yes, a koala is a marsupial, not a bear.

1. **What is the stated main idea of the paragraph?**
   Most people know that kangaroos have pockets.
   One of the most common marsupials is the opossum.
   The classification of animals known as marsupials is made up of mostly
   "pouched" animals.

2. **Think about how marsupials look different from each other.
   Which is one supporting detail?**
   Some other animals have pockets, too.
   A bandicoot can be as large as a rabbit.
   Bandicoots can hop on their back legs.

3. **Think about how marsupials act different from each other.
   Which are two supporting details?**
   A Tasmanian devil preys on animals larger than itself. A wombat is shy.
   A Tasmanian devil is fierce-looking. Another marsupial looks like a koala.
   A koala is a marsupial. A wombat can dig a burrow 100 feet long.

Snorkeling

**Read the paragraph. Underline the stated main idea.
Then draw a line from the name of each piece of
equipment to a supporting detail you learned about it.**

Snorkeling is an activity that allows swimmers to observe underwater life without having to attend scuba diving classes. In order to snorkel, swimmers need a few pieces of simple equipment. First, they must have a snorkel for breathing. This device consists of a tube that extends from the swimmer's mouth to the air above the surface of the water. A snorkeling mask keeps water out of the swimmer's eyes and helps the eyes focus underwater. Swim fins, sometimes called flippers, allow snorkelers to swim easier and faster. If the water is cold, the snorkeler may wear a wetsuit. Some snorkelers also wear a snorkeling vest. The vest is filled with air so that the swimmer can float and use less energy.

Snorkeling Equipment	Supporting Details
wetsuit	**to breathe**
swim fins	**to stay warm**
snorkel	**to protect eyes**
snorkeling vest	**to swim faster**
snorkeling mask	**to float**

Butterflies

Read the paragraph.

Butterflies have many predators, including birds, snakes, lizards, and other insects. However, butterflies have several ways to protect themselves from their enemies. For example, a butterfly may be poisonous. The monarch caterpillar eats milkweed, which makes it poisonous when it turns into a butterfly. Another butterfly benefits from this arrangement as well. The viceroy butterfly looks very much like the monarch, so birds avoid it, too. Several butterflies use camouflage to avoid predators. The Indian leaf butterfly blends into its surroundings by looking like a dead leaf. Some butterflies have patterns on their wings that scare away enemies. A buckeye's wings have large spots that look like giant eyes. These spots can trick a predator into thinking it's facing a dangerous animal instead of a fragile butterfly!

Write the stated main idea. _____

Write one supporting detail about how each butterfly protects itself from predators.

Monarch: _____

Viceroy: _____

Indian leaf: _____

Buckeye: _____

Assessment

Read the paragraph. Then fill in the boxes with the stated main idea and supporting details.

Many people are annoyed when the swimming pool closes or a sports event is cancelled due to an approaching storm. However, lightning is the second leading cause of storm deaths in the United States. Lightning also causes many serious injuries each year. What can you do to stay safe? According to the National Weather Service, people should go inside at the first roll of thunder. Once inside, stay away from electrical appliances, including corded phones, TVs, and computers, and stay out of the bathtub or shower. If you can't get to a building, get in a car and roll up the windows. If you MUST stay outside, stay off hills. Stay out of water and open fields. Stay away from metal fences and poles, and NEVER seek shelter under a tree. Once you find a spot, crouch down into a small ball. Remember—lightning can be dangerous!

Stated Main Idea	Supporting Details

Overview Identifying Unstated Main Idea and Supporting Details

Directions and Sample Answers for Activity Pages

Day 1	See "Provide a Real-World Example" below.
Day 2	Read and discuss the paragraph. Then ask students to draw a circle around the best answers. (**1:** They describe how polar bears move about on icy surfaces. **2:** Polar bears have special ways to get across ice.)
Day 3	Read and discuss the paragraph. Then ask students to write about tugboats. (**1:** push or pull large ships into a harbor, tow disabled ships and barges in for repairs, move small barges carrying construction equipment and supplies. **2:** Tugboats are important workers in a harbor.)
Day 4	Read and discuss the paragraph. Then ask students to color the circle in front of each supporting detail and write an unstated main idea. (**Supporting Details:** peanut butter, table knife, kitchen, string, slice of bread, watch birds enjoy their snack, cookie cutter, drinking straw. **Unstated Main Idea:** You can make a bird feeder using items you already have in your home.)
Day 5	Read the paragraph together. Ask students to record the supporting details, figure out what they have in common, and use the information to write the unstated main idea. Afterward, meet individually with students to discuss their results. Use their responses to plan further instruction and review. (**Supporting Details:** money was scarce, workers were already constructing another bridge, took years to get approval, strong ocean currents, dizziness, powerful winds, constant fog, dangerous. **Unstated Main Idea:** Building the Golden Gate Bridge was a challenge.)

Provide a Real-World Example

◆ Hand out the Day 1 activity page.

◆ **Say:** *Many people want to become doctors. In order to become a doctor, you must first graduate from a four-year college or university. Next, you must pass the medical school admissions test. If you are accepted, you must complete four years of medical school and exams. Then, you must complete three years of residency and take your final exams.* Ask students to complete these supporting details on the page.

◆ **Say:** *We can figure out what these details have in common and use that information to determine a main idea. Each detail is a step in the process of becoming a doctor, so the main idea could be that it takes a long time to become a doctor.* Allow time for students to discuss other possible main ideas and choose one to record.

◆ Explain that students can also use supporting details to figure out an unstated main idea when they read. Write the following on chart paper:

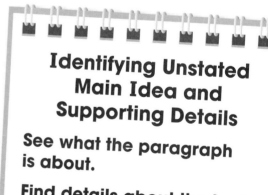

Identifying Unstated Main Idea and Supporting Details

See what the paragraph is about.

Find details about the topic.

Figure out what the details have in common.

Use that information to determine an unstated main idea.

Becoming a Doctor

**Listen to the example.
Then complete the
supporting details.**

Supporting Details

You must graduate from a four-year _____ or _____.

You must pass the _____ admissions test.

You must complete _____ years of medical school and exams.

You must complete _____ years of residency and take your final _____.

Complete the unstated main idea.

Unstated Main Idea

It takes _____ to become a doctor.

Polar Bears on Ice

Read the paragraph. Then draw a circle around the best answer to each question.

Polar bears live in the Arctic where their environment is snowy and icy. They like to be near the ocean and are excellent swimmers. However, walking is not as easy for them, especially if they have to walk over ice. When a polar bear comes to an icy area, it curves its legs and turns in its front paws. Walking bow-legged and pigeon-toed keeps the bear from losing its balance and slipping. Sometimes a polar bear must go down a slick, icy slope. What does it do then? It lies on its stomach and stretches its legs out straight. Then it slides, using its own body for a sled.

1. What do the details in the paragraph have in common?

They describe how polar bears walk.

They describe how polar bears swim.

They describe the polar bears' environment.

They describe how polar bears move about on icy surfaces.

2. What is the unstated main idea of the paragraph?

The cold, icy Arctic has many polar bears.

Polar bears have special ways to get across ice.

Polar bears are better at swimming than walking.

The polar bears' environment has many slick, icy slopes.

Tough Tugs

Read the paragraph. Then write about tugboats.

Working in harbors, tugboats help ocean liners, tankers, barges, and other large sea-going ships. Although a big ship is able to move forward and backward in the harbor, it can't move sideways. To remedy this problem, two tugboats meet the ship and push or pull it in. Each tug is attached to the ship by a line, one on the ship's side and one behind the ship. Tugboats have other jobs, too. Sometimes a tugboat uses a towing cable to tow a disabled ship or barge in for repairs. A tugboat may also work at a construction site that is near a body of water by moving small barges carrying equipment and supplies from place to place.

1. Write details about tugboats.

_____

_____

_____

_____

2. Write an unstated main idea about tugboats.

_____

_____

Homemade Birdfeeder

Read the paragraph. Color the circle in front of each supporting detail. Then write an unstated main idea.

Look around your kitchen. Do you have a slice of bread, a cookie cutter, some string, a drinking straw, some peanut butter, and a table knife? Use the cookie cutter to cut a fun shape from the bread. Poke a hole through the top of the bread with the straw, and tie a piece of string through it. Then, allow time for the bread to dry out and stiffen a bit. When the bread is ready, spread peanut butter on one side with the table knife. If you have some birdseed, you can pour some on a plate and press the peanut-buttered side of the bread into it. If not, you're ready to proceed to the final step. Find a low tree branch and hang your bread on it. Then, sit back and watch the birds enjoy their snack!

Supporting Details

○ peanut butter
○ cut and poke
○ table knife
○ kitchen
○ tie and hang
○ string
○ dry and stiffen
○ slice of bread
○ watch birds enjoy their snack
○ pour and press
○ spread on one side
○ cookie cutter
○ proceed to the final step
○ drinking straw

Unstated Main Idea

_____

_____

Assessment

**Read the paragraph. Then fill in the boxes with
the supporting details and unstated main idea.**

    Engineer Joseph Strauss dreamed of building a
bridge to link San Francisco with Marin County,
California. However, it was the time of the Great
Depression, and money was scarce. Besides that,
workers were already constructing the San Francisco Bay Bridge. Strauss finally realized
his dream in 1933 when the local government approved his plan. Then, the real work
began. Engineers had to figure out how to secure the towers of the bridge in strong,
heavy ocean currents. Bridge workers had to endure dizziness, powerful winds, and
constant fog. Since the work was so dangerous, Strauss insisted on providing a safety
net that stretched from one end of the bridge to the other. Miraculously, Strauss and his
engineers and workers completed the magnificent Golden Gate Bridge in only four years.

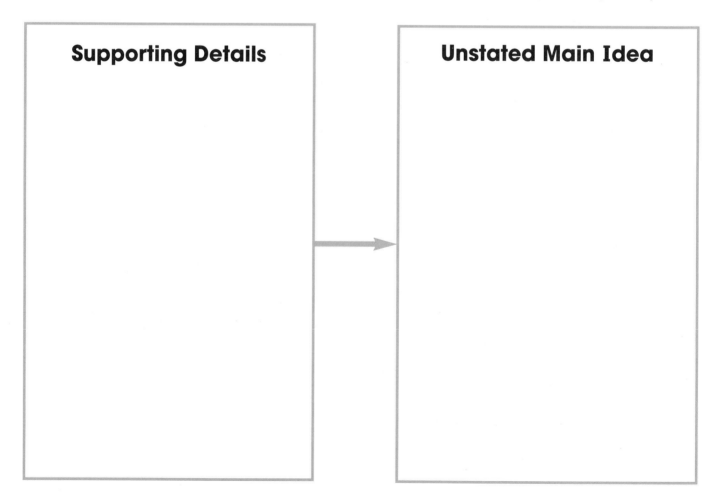

Supporting Details

Unstated Main Idea

Overview Summarizing Fiction

Directions and Sample Answers for Activity Pages

Day 1	See "Provide a Real-World Example" below.
Day 2	Read and discuss the story. Then ask students to draw a circle around the best answers. (**1:** A fox wanted some cheese that a crow had. The fox asked if the crow had a lovely voice. The crow opened her mouth to sing and dropped the cheese. The fox got the cheese. **2:** A fox tricks a crow so he can get her cheese.)
Day 3	Read and discuss the story. Then ask students to underline the big ideas and write a summary. (**Big Ideas:** extra practices; be prepared; work the hardest; get up early to practice on their own before school; read soccer books; watch professional games. **Summary:** The Hawks' hard work pays off when they win the league championship.)
Day 4	Read and discuss the story. Then ask students to cross out the sentences that don't belong. (**Big Ideas:** Cross out 2, 5, 6, and 8. **Summary:** Cross out 1 and 2.)
Day 5	Read the story together. Ask students to record the big ideas and a summary on their graphic organizers. Afterward, meet individually with students to discuss their results. Use their responses to plan further instruction and review. (**Big Ideas:** walked down the alley; heard a noise; saw something in a dark corner ahead; thought it might be a bear; creature came out of the shadows; Peter said, "Hi, guys!" **Summary:** Two boys are frightened by something in the alley, but it turns out to be their friend.)

Provide a Real-World Example

◆ Hand out the Day 1 activity page.

◆ **Say:** *Teachers do many things before the first day of school. They go to meetings. They unpack supplies and set up their classrooms. Then they plan their lessons. Let's think about the big ideas. Teachers go to (meetings). They unpack . . . (supplies). They set up their . . . (classrooms). They plan their . . . (lessons).* Allow time for students to record these activities under **Big Ideas.**

◆ **Say:** *I can summarize what teachers do in one sentence:* Teachers must spend time going to meetings and preparing for the first day of school. Allow time for students to complete the summary.

◆ **Say:** *Students do many things before the first day of school, too.* Invite student partners to record several big ideas and then compose a summary. Allow time for partners to share their summaries with the class.

◆ Explain that students can also summarize stories they read. Write the following on chart paper:

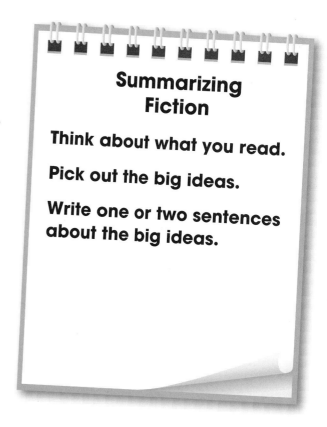

Summarizing Fiction

Think about what you read.

Pick out the big ideas.

Write one or two sentences about the big ideas.

Starting School

Listen to the example. Then write the big ideas and summaries below.

Big Ideas about Teachers

Teachers go to _____.

They unpack _____.

They set up their _____.

They plan their _____.

Summary

Teachers must spend _____ going to _____

and _____ for the first day of _____.

Big Ideas about Students

_____

_____

_____

_____

_____

Summary

_____

_____

The Fox and the Crow

Read the story. Then draw a circle around the best answers.

A fox was strolling through the woods one day when he spied a crow. The crow snatched a piece of cheese from the ground and then flew to the top of a tree. The fox wanted that cheese.

"Good afternoon, Miss Crow," the fox called. "You're looking especially pretty today."

The crow smiled a wide crow smile but still managed to hold the cheese in her mouth.

"You're such a beautiful bird," the fox continued. "You have such stunning, glossy feathers."

The crow slid the cheese to the corner of her mouth. "Yes, I know," she replied.

"Your exquisite dark eyes sparkle," said the fox. "I wonder . . . is your voice as lovely as you are?"

Wanting to show off her voice, the crow opened her mouth to sing. Out fell the cheese. "Good-bye!" called the fox as he ran off with the delectable snack.

1. What are the story's big ideas?

A fox was strolling through the woods.

A crow was at the top of a tree.

A fox wanted some cheese that a crow had.

The crow was pretty.

The fox thought the crow was pretty.

The crow had a lovely voice.

The fox asked if the crow had a lovely voice.

The crow opened her mouth to sing and dropped the cheese.

The fox got the cheese.

2. Which sentence best summarizes the story?

Foxes and crows both like cheese.

A fox tricks a crow so he can get her cheese.

A crow gives a fox some cheese so she can sing for him.

Team Supreme

**Read the story. Draw a line under the big ideas.
Then write a summary.**

"Hey, Paul," Tony called, running up to his friend. "The last soccer game of the season is Saturday afternoon. The team that wins will be the league champions, so Coach Brooks wants to have extra practices this week."

"I'm all for it," Paul said. "We've got to be prepared to face the Eagles. They're good."

"The Hawks can beat them!" Tony said. "We have talent, but we also work the hardest."

"I know," said Paul. "All our players get up early to practice on their own before school."

"We read soccer books and watch professional games to learn more, too," Tony said. "See you at practice!"

On Saturday night, Tony and Paul celebrated their league championship at the Pizza Palace with Coach Brooks and their teammates. "I ordered Supreme Pizzas for the Team Supreme!" said the coach.

Summary

_____

_____

_____

Meetinghouse

Read the story. In the first box, cross out the sentences that are not big ideas. In the second box, cross out the sentences that are not the best summary.

The year was 1650 in colonial America. Seth and his family walked to the meetinghouse. "I like Sundays," said Seth. "No chores!"

Mother smiled. "Hopefully, you can make it through the morning without getting into trouble!"

The church watchman greeted them sternly. He held a long pole with a wooden knob on one end and a squirrel tail on the other. Seth knew what THAT was for!

Soon, Seth's head began to nod. The watchman tapped him with the knob. Later, a man in the front row began snoring. Seth grinned and leaned toward his mother as the watchman tickled the man's nose with the tail. Then Seth frowned and sat up straight. Anyone caught smiling or whispering had to pay money.

After the service, Seth breathed a sign of relief. "Would you like to go fishing this afternoon?" asked Seth's father.

"Sure!" said Seth. "After my nap!"

Big Ideas	**Summary**
1. Seth and his parents went to the meetinghouse on Sundays.	1. Some people went to the meetinghouse on Sunday in colonial days.
2. Seth didn't have to do chores on Sundays.	
3. Sometimes Seth got in trouble at the meetinghouse.	2. The church watchman had an important job to do at the colonial meetinghouse.
4. The meetinghouse had a stern watchman with a long pole.	
5. Seth almost fell asleep at the meetinghouse.	3. A colonial boy knew he was expected to be alert, serious, and quiet at the meetinghouse.
6. Seth thought it was funny to see the watchman tickle a man's nose to wake him up.	
7. Seth sat up straight and didn't smile or whisper so he wouldn't have to pay money.	
8. Seth was tired after the meetinghouse.	

Assessment

Read the story. Then write the big ideas and a summary in the boxes.

Miguel and Brian often walked the short distance down the alley to their friend Peter's house. Tonight they were going to teach Peter to play chess. Miguel heard the noise first. "It's just the wind rattling something," Brian told his brother.

"I don't think so," Miguel whispered. He pointed to a dark corner ahead. "There's something there—it looks like an animal!"

Brian felt his heart beat fast. "What if it's a bear? People have reported seeing bears around their trash cans lately. What should we do?"

"I don't know," Miguel answered, his voice trembling.

Suddenly, the creature came out of the shadows. The boys froze, unable to run. "Hi, guys!" said Peter.

Brian and Miguel took a deep breath and then burst into laughter. "Next time you're coming to OUR house to play chess," Brian said.

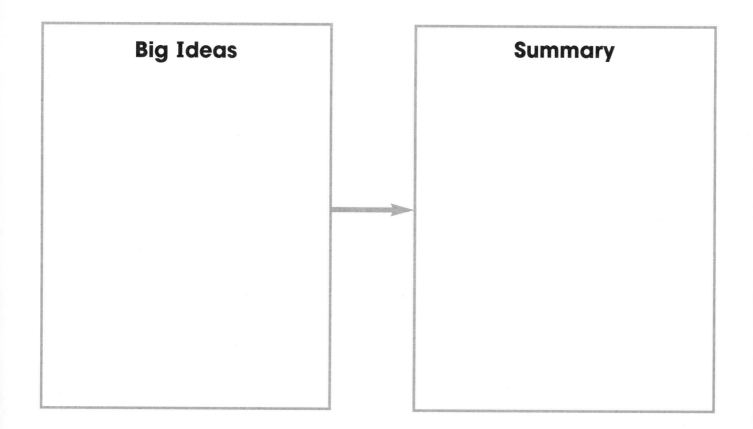

Big Ideas	**Summary**

Overview Summarizing Nonfiction

Directions and Sample Answers for Activity Pages

Day 1	See "Provide a Real-World Example" below.
Day 2	Read and discuss the passage. Then ask students to draw a circle around the best answers. (**1:** 1896; gold in the Yukon Territory of Canada; gold seekers rushed; most found no gold. **2:** Gold seekers rushed to the Yukon in 1896, but few found gold.)
Day 3	Read and discuss the passage. Then ask students to fill in the blanks to complete the sentences. (**Big Ideas:** is very tall and heavy; has a long neck and legs; doesn't have to lie down to sleep; has special blood vessels in its neck to keep it from fainting when it gets a drink; can defend itself with its long, strong legs. **Summary:** A giraffe has unique abilities and body features that allow it to sleep, drink, and defend itself despite its unusual size and shape.)
Day 4	Read and discuss the passage. Then ask students to highlight the big ideas and summary. (**Big Ideas:** She began painting pictures when she was 76 years old. She became a famous artist known as Grandma Moses. **Summary:** Grandma Moses started painting at age 76 and became a famous artist.)
Day 5	Read the passage together. Ask students to record the big ideas and a summary on their graphic organizers. Afterward, meet individually with students to discuss their results. Use their responses to plan further instruction and review. (**Big Ideas:** grow in dry areas; stems are perfect for storing rainwater; stems' waxy coating keeps the water from evaporating; long roots absorb water from the soil; short roots absorb the dew; water does not evaporate from spines; spines protect the cactus from predators. **Summary:** Cactus plants have special features that allow them to live in dry areas.)

Provide a Real-World Example

◆ Hand out the Day 1 activity page.

◆ **Say:** *My friend just got a pet iguana. She feeds it a balanced diet of particular fruits and vegetables and sometimes a little bit of boiled egg whites. She has to mix the fruits and vegetables in a food processor so the iguana will eat everything. If she doesn't, it will pick out what it likes best and leave the rest.*

◆ Ask students to circle each big idea. (*an iguana; balanced diet; particular fruits; particular vegetables; mix in a food processor so the iguana will eat everything*)

◆ **Ask:** *How can we use the big ideas to summarize this information in one sentence?* Together, compose a summary, such as "*To make sure your pet iguana has a balanced diet, choose the right fruits and vegetables and mix them in a food processor.*"

◆ Explain that students can also summarize when they read. Write the following on chart paper:

Summarizing Nonfiction

Think about what you read.

Pick out the big ideas.

Write one or two sentences about the big ideas.

Pet Iguana

**Listen. Circle the big ideas.
Then write a summary.**

Big Ideas

a friend

a pet

an iguana

balanced diet

particular fruits

particular vegetables

sometimes a little bit of boiled egg whites

mix in a food processor so the iguana will eat everything

picks out what it likes best

leaves the rest

Summary

_____

_____

_____

_____

Rushing for Gold

Read the passage. Then draw a circle around the best answers.

In 1896, three men discovered gold in what is now called the Yukon Territory of Canada. When gold seekers heard this news, they rushed to the area by the thousands. Some 100,000 "stampeders" descended on the small settlements of Skagwag and Dyea in Alaska. From there, they trudged through hazardous mountain passes with their supplies to reach Bennett Lake. Those surviving the trek then built boats for a trip of over 500 miles on the Yukon River to get to the gold fields. Most miners found no gold. By 1900, the largest gold rush in North America was over, and most of the would-be millionaires were broke.

1. What are the big ideas?

1896

three men

gold in the Yukon Territory of Canada

news

gold seekers rushed

100,000 stampeders

Skagwag and Dyea

hazardous mountain passes

supplies

Bennett Lake

built boats

500 miles on the Yukon River

most found no gold

1900

largest gold rush in North America

would-be millionaires were broke

2. Which sentence best summarizes the passage?

Skagwag and Dyea are the best places to find gold in Alaska.

People should not try to find gold, because they will probably go broke.

Gold seekers rushed to the Yukon in 1896, but few found gold.

Giraffes

Read the passage. Then complete the sentences.

Measuring 18 feet from the top of its head, the giraffe is the
tallest animal on earth. In addition, male giraffes can weigh 3,000
pounds! Because of their heavy bodies, adult giraffes have difficulty
lying down, so they sleep standing up. With a 6-foot neck and
6-foot legs, it's not easy for a giraffe to bend over for a drink of
water, either. It could even faint if not for the elastic blood vessels
in its neck. However, a giraffe can go without drinking water for a
long period of time. Giraffes' long, strong legs help them, too.
When necessary, a giraffe will defend itself against a predator with
powerful kicks.

Big Ideas

A giraffe . . .

is very _____ and _____.

has a long _____ and _____.

doesn't have to _____ to sleep.

has special _____ in its neck to keep it from _____
when it gets a drink.

can _____ itself with its long, strong _____.

Summary

A _____ has unique abilities and body features that allow it to

_____, _____, and _____

itself despite its _____ size and shape.

Grandma Moses

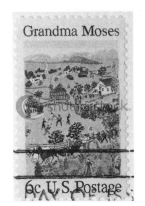

Read the passage. In the first box, use a highlighter to mark the big ideas. In the second box, use a highlighter to mark the best summary.

Anna Mary Robertson Moses was born in 1860 and grew up on a farm in New York State. She enjoyed drawing pictures as a child and made embroidered pictures as an adult. When she was 76 years old, she could no longer embroider because of arthritis in her hands. Instead, she began painting happy scenes from her childhood in a simple, detailed style. Little did she know she would become a famous artist known as Grandma Moses! When an art collector saw her paintings in the window of a drugstore, he bought all of them. Then, he went to her farm and bought her other fifteen paintings. After an exhibit in 1940, her paintings were in great demand across the United States and throughout Europe.

Big Ideas

Anna Mary Robertson Moses was born in 1860.

She grew up on a farm in New York State.

She liked to make embroidered pictures.

She got arthritis in her hands.

She began painting pictures at age 76.

The pictures were of happy scenes that included many details.

She became a famous artist known as Grandma Moses.

An art collector bought her first paintings.

She had an exhibit in 1940.

People in the United States and Europe wanted her paintings.

Summary

Art collectors often look for paintings in unusual places.

People who get arthritis in their hands often try new hobbies.

People who enjoy drawing pictures as a child often try painting as an adult.

Grandma Moses started painting at age 76 and became a famous artist.

People in the United States and Europe like paintings of happy scenes in a simple, detailed style.

Assessment

Read the passage. Then write the big ideas and a summary in the boxes.

Cactus plants grow in dry areas. How do cacti survive where water is scarce? Several features make the difference between life and death. Their stems are thick and either hollow or spongy—perfect for storing rainwater. In addition, the stems' waxy coating keeps the water from evaporating in the hot sun. Some cacti have long roots that absorb water from the soil, and cacti with short roots absorb the dew that collects on the plant. Instead of leaves, a cactus has spines. Unlike leaves, water does not evaporate from spines. Spines also protect the cactus from predators that want to eat the plant to get its stored water.

Big Ideas	Summary

Overview Comparing and Contrasting in Fiction

Directions and Sample Answers for Activity Pages

Day 1	See "Provide a Real-World Example" below.
Day 2	Read and discuss the story. Ask students to underline the compare-and-contrast signal words in the story. Then ask them to fill in the Venn diagram. (**Signal Words: both, but, too, same, alike. Ramon:** likes rock music, going to a show in the city with his uncle. **Both:** want autographs, have fan magazines, have CDs. **Dan:** likes country music, going to a show at the fair with his mom.)
Day 3	Read and discuss the story. Ask students to mark the chart by placing X's in the appropriate columns to show how Mistress Smith and Anna are alike and different. Then ask them to add one more detail to compare and contrast. (**Mistress Smith:** trusting, likes eggs, kind, cheerful, angry at the peddler. **Anna:** likes eggs, serious, angry at the peddler, suspicious.)
Day 4	Read and discuss the story. Then ask students to mark each statement true or false and correct any false statements. (**1:** True. **2:** False. Grace likes long-sleeved T-shirts. **3:** False. Charlie likes short-sleeved T-shirts. **4:** True. **5:** False. Charlie likes golden retrievers best. **6:** False. Grace likes Scotties best. **7:** False. Charlie wears size large. **8:** False. Grace wears size small. **9:** True.)
Day 5	Read the story together. Ask students to fill in the chart to compare and contrast John and Mo. Afterward, meet individually with students to discuss their results. Use their responses to plan further instruction and review. (**John:** wants to take photos of wildflowers, has binoculars. **John and Mo:** have cameras; walk the same trail; like being outdoors; have the same science teacher. **Mo:** wants to take photos of birds, has a magnifying glass.)

Provide a Real-World Example

◆ Hand out the Day 1 activity page.

◆ **Say:** *I will name some books in our school (or classroom) library. If you have read the book, stand up. If not, remain seated.* Call out several fiction and nonfiction titles.

◆ Explain that discovering books that classmates have read in common is comparing. Discovering books they have read that are different is contrasting.

◆ Invite volunteers to create oral sentences comparing or contrasting themselves to classmates regarding their reading preferences. Write signal words they use on the board, such as *Liza and I* **both** *like to read historical fiction. Ahmaud likes science books, and I like science books,* **too**. *Keagan enjoys long books,* **but** *I like shorter ones. I check out books from a* **different** *section of the library than Alyssa does.*

◆ Give students a few minutes to mingle and fill in the sentences on their pages. Invite them to share their findings.

◆ Explain that students can also compare and contrast when they read stories. Write the following on chart paper:

Comparing and Contrasting in Fiction

Find things in a story that are alike.

Look for compare signal words like *alike, too, both, same,* and *in common*.

Find things in the story that are different.

Look for contrast signal words like *different, but,* and *however*.

I Read, You Read

Listen to the example. Then compare and contrast the books you like to read with your classmates' favorites.

Comparing

_____ and I have both read

_____.

I like to read the _____ genre, and

_____likes to read this genre, too.

Contrasting

My favorite book is _____.

However, _____'s favorite book is

_____.

_____ likes to read in/on the

_____ , but I like to read

in/on the _____.

Music Fans

**Read the story. Draw a line under the
compare-and-contrast signal words.
Then fill in the Venn diagram.**

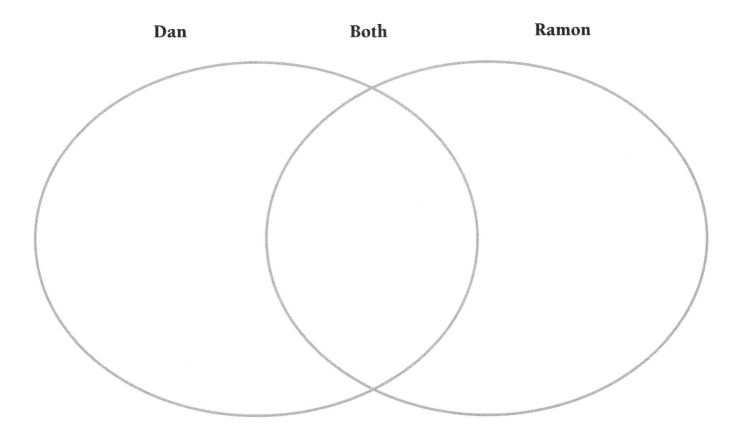

"Guess what?" Ramon asked Dan. "I'm going
to the city to visit my uncle. He has tickets to a
Four Dudes show. It'll be my first rock concert!"

"We're both going to a show!" Dan replied.
"But I'm going to the Billy Cash country music show
at the Greenville Fair. My mom got our tickets last night. I'm going to try
to get Billy's autograph!"

"I hope to get autographs, too," Ramon said. "I read about the Dudes in my fan
magazine. The article said they like to mingle with the crowd."

"I read the same thing about Billy," said Dan. "I'm going to ask him to sign my
magazine. . . . or maybe a CD."

"We're thinking alike," Ramon exclaimed. "I want the Dudes to sign a CD for me!"

Dan	Both	Ramon

Gollywhopper Eggs

Read the story. Then mark the chart to compare and contrast Mistress Smith and Anna. At the bottom of the chart, add one more detail to compare and contrast.

"Gollywhopper eggs! Gollywhopper eggs for sale! Two for a dollar," cried the peddler.

"They're gigantic!" said Mistress Smith. "And brown . . . and hairy!"

"They're also rare," said the peddler. "I traveled to a remote island to find the bird that lays these eggs."

"I'll take two," said Mistress Smith. "I'll cook one for my friend Anna. We both love eggs!"

Mistress Smith took her eggs home. Then she hurried to Anna's house and invited her to come for breakfast the next morning. Anna frowned. "I'm suspicious," she said. "I've never heard of gollywhopper eggs."

Anna arrived at Mistress Smith's house at sunrise. "Let me see the eggs," she demanded. Mistress Smith proudly put them on the table. "Those are coconuts!" Anna exclaimed.

"I don't know what coconuts are," said Mistress Smith. "But I'm angry! I paid a dollar for the eggs."

"I'm angry, too," Anna replied. "That peddler cheated you!"

	Mistress Smith	**Anna**
trusting		
likes eggs		
kind		
serious		
travels to a remote island		
cheerful		
angry at the peddler		
suspicious		
eats gollywhopper eggs		

T-Shirts for a Cause

**Read the story. Then mark each statement true (T) or false (F).
If the statement is false, write a true statement on the line.**

"Hi, Grace!" said Charlie. "What are you doing at the animal shelter?"

"I came to buy a T-shirt," said Grace. "The shelter is selling them to raise money for abandoned animals. I'm getting a black one with long sleeves."

"That's why I came, too," said Charlie. "Mine will be black like yours, but I like short sleeves. Look at this shirt with a golden retriever on it. That's my favorite dog. I'm buying it!"

"We'll both have dog shirts, but mine will have a Scottie on it," said Grace.

"The T-shirts are selling fast," said Charlie. "I hope there's a large size left."

"I'm lucky . . . I found the last Scottie shirt sized small!" exclaimed Grace.

Grace and Charlie . . .

1. ____ both like black T-shirts _____

2. ____ both like long-sleeved T-shirts _____

3. ____ both like short-sleeved T-shirts _____

4. ____ both like dogs _____

5. ____ both like golden retrievers best _____

6. ____ both like Scotties best _____

7. ____ both wear size large _____

8. ____ both wear size small _____

9. ____ both care about abandoned animals_____

Assessment

Read the story. Then fill in the chart to show how John and Mo are alike and different.

"Thanks for coming to the nature park with me, Mo," said John. "I couldn't wait to use my new camera. I promised my mom I'd get shots of some of these wildflowers. I might use them in my science report, too."

"I'm going to take bird photos for my report," said Mo as he turned on his camera. "We can walk the same trail and look for both."

"Sure thing," said John. "I'm glad we both like being outdoors. Maybe we can work on our science reports together, too. I don't think Ms. Jackson would mind."

Mo took a magnifying glass out of his pocket. "You can borrow this for a close-up look at the flowers," he said.

"Thanks!" said John. He reached into his backpack. "And you can borrow my binoculars to search for birds in the distance."

John	John and Mo	Mo

Overview Comparing and Contrasting in Nonfiction

Directions and Sample Answers for Activity Pages

Day 1	See "Provide a Real-World Example" below.
Day 2	Read and discuss the passage. Ask students to underline the compare-and-contrast signal words in the passage. Then ask them to fill in the Venn diagram. (**Signal Words: both, one, other, unlike, same, but, different, while, differ. Susan B. Anthony coin:** silver, grooved edge, narrower border. **Both:** worth one dollar, picture of a woman on the front, same diameter. **Sacagawea coin:** golden color, smooth edge, wider border.)
Day 3	Read and discuss the passage. Then ask students to answer the questions. (**1:** Both have wings and long, strong back legs. **2:** Crickets usually sing at night, but grasshoppers usually sing in the day. **3:** Both are expert jumpers. Both blend in with their environments. **4:** They're in different families in the animal world. Only grasshoppers fly. Grasshoppers are green, but crickets are brown.)
Day 4	Read and discuss the passage. Then ask students to circle the best answers. (**1:** apothecary. **2:** pharmacist. **3:** both. **4:** both. **5:** apothecary. **6:** apothecary. **7:** apothecary. **8:** apothecary. **9:** pharmacist. **10:** both.)
Day 5	Read the two advertisements together. Ask students to fill in the chart to compare and contrast the camps. Afterward, meet individually with students to discuss their results. Use their responses to plan further instruction and review. (**Camp Minnerocka:** open in June and August, crafts, music, tents, eat by campfire. **Both camps:** open in July, ages 10–12, sports, $150 per week. **Forest Hollow Sports Camp:** air-conditioned cabins, cafeteria-style meals, $500 for whole month.)

Provide a Real-World Example

◆ Hand out the Day 1 activity page.

◆ **Say:** *Recently, I wanted to buy a gift for a friend. I thought about going to a shop I like, and I thought about going to the mall. I compared the two places by thinking of ways they are alike. I contrasted them by thinking of ways they are different.*

◆ Read the first sentence and ask students to circle the word **but**. **Say:** *But is a signal word we use to contrast two things.* Then ask students to put a check mark in the chart to show that the sizes of the stores are different.

◆ Repeat the process with the other sentences, asking volunteers to identify the signal words. Point out that **whereas** and **while** signal contrasts, and **both** signals a comparison.

◆ Explain that students can also compare and contrast when they read. Write the following on chart paper:

Comparing and Contrasting in Nonfiction

Find things in a passage that are alike.

Look for compare signal words like *too, both, alike,* and *same*.

Find things in the passage that are different.

Look for contrast signal words like *but, whereas, however, while, different, unlike,* and *on the other hand*.

Shop or Mall?

Read the passage. Then use the chart to compare and contrast.

The shop is small, but the mall is large.

I can park right in front of the shop, whereas the mall has a large, crowded parking lot.

The shop mainly sells gift items, while the mall has many types of merchandise.

The shop and the mall both have unique items to buy.

	Same	**Different**
size		
parking area		
types of merchandise		
availability of unique items		

Dollar Coins

Read the passage. Draw a line under the compare-and-contrast signal words. Then fill in the Venn diagram.

The United States has two coins in circulation that are worth one dollar each. Both coins have a picture of a woman on the front. One has a picture of Susan B. Anthony, an activist who worked to secure voting rights for women. The other has a picture of Sacagawea, a Native American who guided Lewis and Clark on their western expedition. Unlike the Susan B. Anthony coin, which is silver, the Sacagawea coin is a golden color. The coins have the same diameter, but the edges of the coins are different. While the Susan B. Anthony coin has a grooved edge, the Sacagewea coin has a smooth edge. Another way the coins differ is their border—the Sacagawea coin's border is wider.

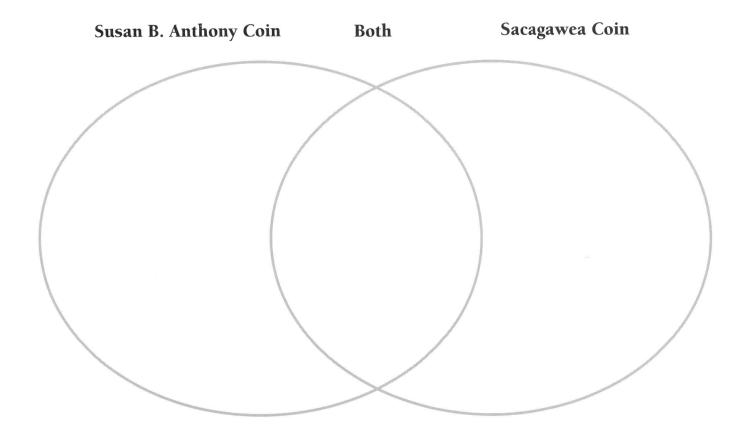

Susan B. Anthony Coin   **Both**   **Sacagawea Coin**

Crickets and Grasshoppers

Read the passage. Then answer the questions.

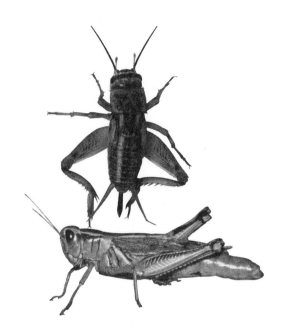

Although crickets and grasshoppers are alike in many ways, they are in different families in the animal world. Both insects make musical sounds. We usually hear cricket songs at night, while a grasshopper usually sings in the daytime. Crickets and grasshoppers both have wings, but only grasshoppers fly. Both insects have long, strong back legs, which make them expert jumpers. Grasshoppers are green so they can blend in with their grassy environment. On the other hand, crickets are brown so they can blend in with the darkness of night.

1. How are the insects' bodies similar?

_____

2. How are the insects' habits different?

_____

3. How else are the two insects alike?

_____

4. How else are the two insects different?

_____

Apothecaries and Pharmacists

Read the passage. Then circle the correct word or words for each description.

People in colonial America could buy medicines from an apothecary (uh-PAH-thuh-keh-ree). Today, we buy medicines from a pharmacist. Besides selling medicines, apothecaries often treated sick and injured people and performed surgery. However, doctors and surgeons provide this type of care today. Unlike most pharmacists, apothecaries actually made the medicines. They put the ingredients in a bowl called a mortar, and crushed and mixed them together with a tool called a pestle. In modern times, drug companies make nearly all the medicines that pharmacists sell. Apothecaries sold items other than medicines, including spices, toothbrushes, and candles. Pharmacists sell a variety of items, too.

1. work in colonial America	apothecary	pharmacist	both
2. work today	apothecary	pharmacist	both
3. sell medicines	apothecary	pharmacist	both
4. operate a store	apothecary	pharmacist	both
5. treat sick and injured people	apothecary	pharmacist	both
6. perform surgeries	apothecary	pharmacist	both
7. make medicines	apothecary	pharmacist	both
8. use a mortar and pestle	apothecary	pharmacist	both
9. get medicines from drug companies	apothecary	pharmacist	both
10. sell items beside medicine	apothecary	pharmacist	both

Assessment

Read the two advertisements. Then fill in the chart to show how the two summer camps are alike and different.

Camp Minnerocka
Open June, July,
and August
Ages 10–12
Sports! Crafts! Music!
Sleep in tents!
Eat by the campfire!
Cost: $150 per week

Forest Hollow Sports Camp
July 1–31
Ages 10–12
Basketball, baseball,
soccer, swimming
Air-conditioned cabins!
Cafeteria-style meals!
Cost: $150 per week, or $500
for the whole month

Camp Minnerocka	Both Camps	Forest Hollow Sports Camp

Overview Identifying Cause and Effect in Fiction

Directions and Sample Answers for Activity Pages

Day 1	See "Provide a Real-World Example" below.
Day 2	Read and discuss the story. Then ask students to underline the cause-and-effect signal words and answer the questions. (**Signal Words: because, as a result, so, why. 1:** He was worried because Heron was bigger and ate more fish. **2:** He stopped to admire the beautiful flowers and sip their delicious nectar. **3:** He became so full and fat he could barely fly. **4:** He reached the lake before Hummingbird did. **5:** He won the race. **6:** He found a new food that tasted even better than fish.)
Day 3	Read and discuss the story. Then ask students to fill in the missing causes and effects. (**1:** They're going to do it together at Betsy's house. **2:** Molly pets Betsy's cat, Peplo. **3:** Molly begins coughing and rubbing her eyes. **4:** She doesn't want Molly to feel miserable.)
Day 4	Read and discuss the story. Then ask students to fill in the graphic organizer. (**1:** family must turn up heat. **2:** ice on trees. **3:** snowdrifts block roads. **4:** power outage. **5:** no school.)
Day 5	Read the story together. Ask students to record three causes and effects on their graphic organizers. Afterward, meet individually with students to discuss their results. Use their responses to plan further instruction and review. (**Cause:** The road has a patch of gravel. **Effect:** Roger skids and lands in the ditch. **Cause:** People sometimes get hurt on bike trips. **Effect:** Dad carries a first-aid kit in his pack. **Cause:** Roger only has a few scratches. **Effect:** He doesn't require first aid. **Cause:** Dad runs over glass at the picnic area. **Effect:** He gets a flat tire. **Cause:** People sometimes have bike problems on bike trips. **Effect:** Dad carries a bike first-aid kit in his pack.)

Provide a Real-World Example

◆ Hand out the Day 1 activity page.

◆ Invite volunteers to role-play a situation in which they miss a favorite activity because they have to clean their room. Ask classmates to state the cause, or reason, and the effect, or what happened. Encourage them to use cause-and-effect signal words, such as *Abdullah's room was messy, **so** he had to clean it instead of watching TV* or *Alayna missed the basketball game **since** she had to clean her room.* Allow time for students to write the words **cause** and **effect** under the appropriate boxes.

◆ Repeat the process with two additional home scenarios. (The dog needs to go for a walk. Today is Dad's birthday.)

◆ Explain that students can also identify cause-and-effect relationships when they read stories. Write the following on chart paper:

Identifying Cause and Effect in Fiction

Think about what made something happen. What was the cause, or reason?

Think about what happened. What was the effect, or result?

Look for cause-and-effect signal words like *because, since, why*, and *as a result*.

Home Events

**Look at each picture and draw or write a possible effect.
Then label each box** *cause* **or** *effect*.

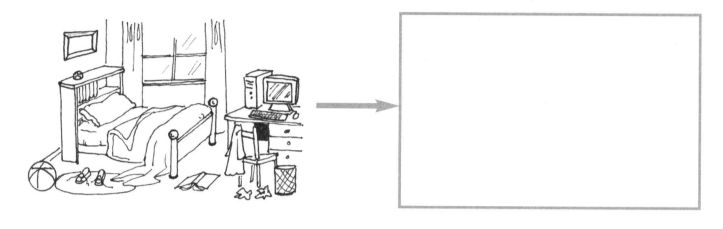

_____

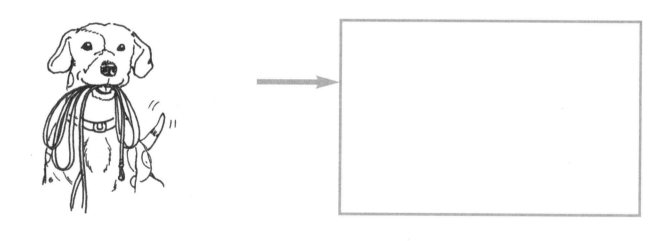

_____

Heron and Hummingbird

Read the story. Draw a line under the cause-and-effect signal words. Then answer the questions.

Long ago, Heron and Hummingbird both loved to eat fish. Because Heron was so much larger, he ate more fish. This worried Hummingbird. "Let's have a race," Hummingbird proposed. "The winner will get all the fish on Earth."

"You're on!" Heron agreed. "We'll race to Faraway Lake. Whoever catches the first fish there is the winner."

Heron flew steadily all the next day, but Hummingbird kept stopping to admire the beautiful flowers and sip their delicious nectar. As a result, he soon became so full and fat he could barely fly.

When Hummingbird finally reached the lake, Heron was dining on the fish he had caught. "You won, so you get all the fish on Earth," said Hummingbird. "But I won, too. I found a new food that tastes even better than fish!" And that is why herons eat fish and hummingbirds eat nectar to this very day.

1. What caused Hummingbird to propose a race?

_____

2. Why did Hummingbird keep stopping during the race?

_____

3. What happened when Hummingbird drank nectar?

_____

4. What was the result of Heron's steady flying?

_____

5. Why did Heron get all the fish on Earth?

_____

6. Why did Hummingbird say he won, too?

_____

Peplo

Read the story. Then fill in the missing causes and effects.

"Hi, Molly!" said Betsy as she answered the doorbell. "I'm glad we can do our math homework together. And look—I have a new cat! Her name is Peplo."

"She's beautiful," Molly said, petting Peplo's long fur. As the girls walked up the stairs, Molly sneezed. "Uh-oh," she said. "I forgot to tell you—I'm allergic to cats!"

The girls went into Betsy's room, and Peplo followed them. Soon, Molly began coughing and rubbing her eyes. Betsy picked up her pet and took her back downstairs. "I don't want you to feel miserable," Betsy said when she returned. "Besides, Peplo doesn't need to learn math!"

1. **Cause:** Betsy and Molly have math homework.

   Effect: _____

2. **Cause:** _____

   Effect: Molly sneezes.

3. **Cause:** Peplo follows the girls into Betsy's room.

   Effect: _____

4. **Cause:** _____

   Effect: Betsy takes Peplo back downstairs.

Blizzard!

Sometimes one cause can have many effects, which in turn cause other things to happen. Read the story. Then fill in the missing boxes on the graphic organizer.

The Wilson family listened to the wind whistling. Cold air was creeping in around the windows, so Mom turned up the heat. "The weather man said this is the worst blizzard of the season," she said.

"Look out back," said Dad. "With so much ice on the trees, some of the branches have broken."

"Do you think we'll have school tomorrow, Mom?" Jamie asked.

"I doubt it," Mom replied. "Since snowdrifts have blocked several roads, no vehicles can get through."

"The wind has blown wires down in some parts of town, too," Dad added. "When that happens, we can have a power outage."

Just then, all the lights in the Wilson house went off. "I'll get the candles!" said Jamie.

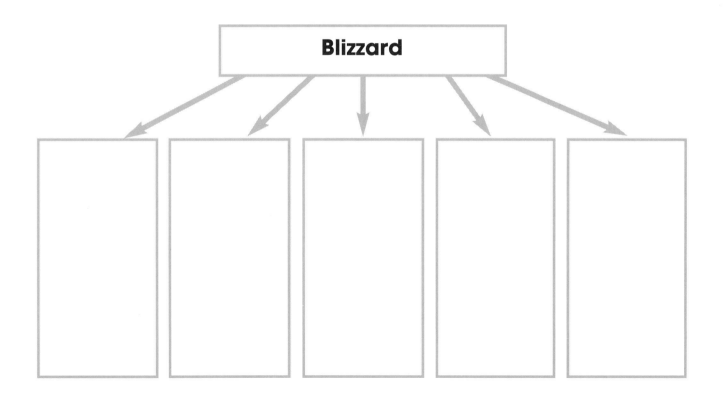

Assessment

Read the story. Then fill in the graphic organizers to show three of the cause-and-effect relationships.

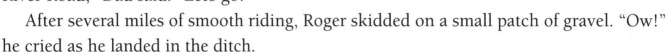

"Are you ready for our bike trip?" asked Dad.

"Ready!" said Roger.

They both put on their backpacks. "We're taking River Road," Dad said. "Let's go!"

After several miles of smooth riding, Roger skidded on a small patch of gravel. "Ow!" he cried as he landed in the ditch.

Dad raced back to Roger. "Are you okay?" he asked. "I have a first-aid kit in my pack."

"I'm okay," Roger answered. "Just a few scratches." He climbed back on his bike and soon forgot all about the mishap.

After breaking for lunch, Dad and Roger headed for the reservoir. They had gone only a short distance when Dad pulled over. "I must have run over some glass at the picnic area, because I've got a flat," he said. "Luckily, I've got my bike first-aid kit in my pack, too!"

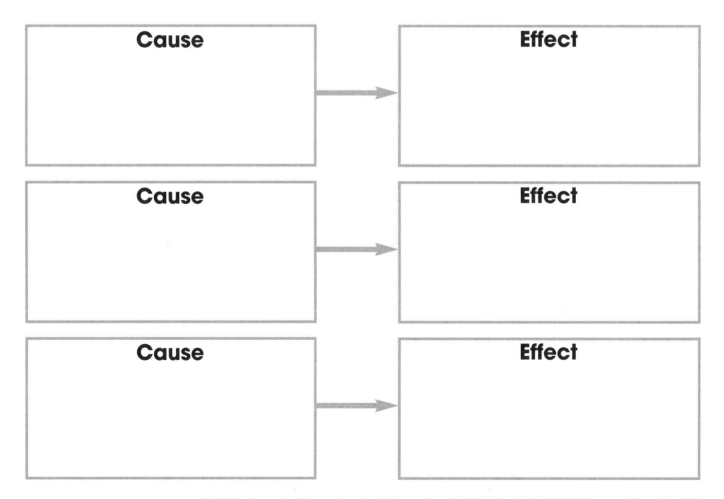

Cause	**Effect**

Cause	**Effect**

Cause	**Effect**

Overview Identifying Cause and Effect in Nonfiction

Directions and Sample Answers for Activity Pages

Day 1	See "Provide a Real-World Example" below.
Day 2	Read and discuss the passage. Then ask students to underline the cause-and-effect signal words and answer the questions. (**Signal Words: if, as a result, since. 1:** It sees a shark, eel, or other enemy. **2:** It sends out a cloud of ink from its sac. **3:** The octopus fights with its arms. **4:** The octopus is able to hold onto its food easily.)
Day 3	Read and discuss the passage. Then ask students to write an effect for each cause. (**1:** A solar eclipse occurs. **2:** People on Earth see only a small ring of light around the moon. **3:** People want to see it. **4:** No one should look at it directly, through binoculars, or through a telescope. **5:** They can view the solar eclipse safely.)
Day 4	Read and discuss the passage. Then ask students to fill in the missing causes and effects. (**1:** People from all over the world plan vacations there. **2:** Many people enjoy rodeos. **3:** They visit Hanauma Bay in Hawaii. **4:** Comstock Lode once produced billions of dollars in gold and silver. **5:** They visit Bryce Canyon National Park and Sequoia National Park. **6:** Death Valley is extremely hot in the summer.)
Day 5	Read the passage together. Ask students to record three causes and effects on their graphic organizers. Afterward, meet individually with students to discuss their results. Use their responses to plan further instruction and review. (**Cause:** Water on Earth is always on the move. **Effect:** The water cycles. **Cause:** The sun heats the water. **Effect:** The water becomes a vapor. **Cause:** The vapor rises into the air. **Effect:** The vapor cools. **Cause:** The vapor cools. **Effect:** The vapor changes back into a liquid state and forms clouds. **Cause:** The clouds get heavy and cannot hold the water. **Effect:** The water falls to Earth as precipitation. **Cause:** The water ends up back in a body of water. **Effect:** The water cycle continues.)

Provide a Real-World Example

◆ Hand out the Day 1 activity page.

◆ Invite volunteers to role-play a situation in which a student needs money to go on a field trip. After each example, ask classmates to state the cause, or reason, and the effect, or what happened. Encourage them to use cause-and-effect signal words, such as *Since Brandon needs money for a field trip, his grandpa is going to pay him to rake the leaves* or *Maya needs five dollars for a field trip, so she's going to skip the movie tonight.* Allow time for students to write or draw one of the effects in the top box on the page. Then ask them to write the words **cause** and **effect** under the appropriate boxes.

◆ Repeat the process with two additional scenarios. (My best friend is moving to another city. I can't find my library book that's due tomorrow.)

◆ Explain that students can also identify cause-and-effect relationships when they read. Write the following on chart paper:

Identifying Cause and Effect in Nonfiction

Think about what made something happen. What was the cause, or reason?

Think about what happened. What was the effect, or result?

Look for cause-and-effect signal words like *because, since, so, if,* and *as a result.*

What Happened?

**Look at each picture and draw or write a possible effect.
Then label each box** *cause* **or** *effect***.**

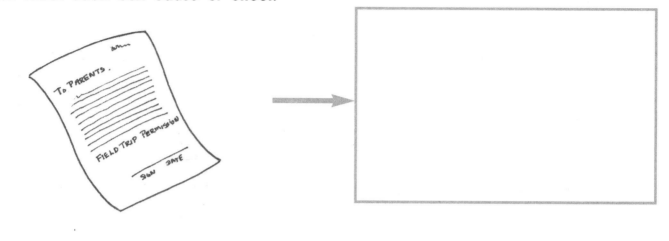

_____   _____

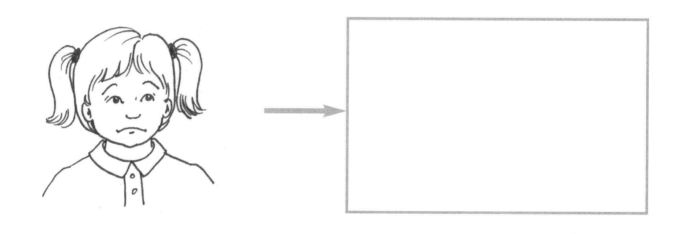

_____   _____

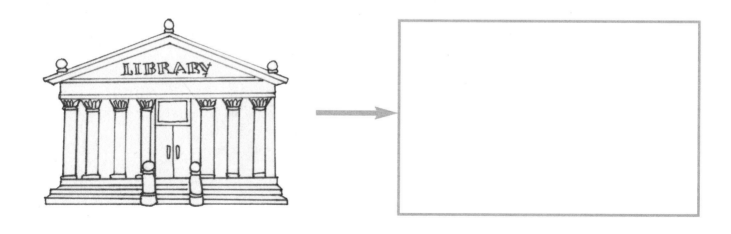

_____   _____

The Octopus

**Read the passage. Draw a line under
the cause-and-effect signal words.
Then answer the questions.**

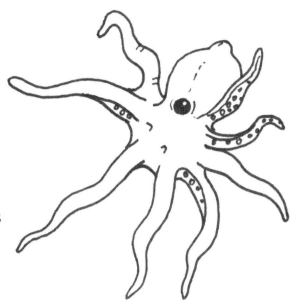

The octopus is a strange-looking sea
animal with eight long, strong arms and a
body shaped like a bag. Hidden in its body
is a sac filled with black ink. If the octopus
sees a shark, eel, or other enemy, it becomes frightened. As a result, it sends out
a cloud of ink from its sac. Then, if the
enemy attacks, the octopus fights with its arms. The octopus also uses its arms to grab
prey, such as crabs or mollusks. Since each arm has two rows of suction cups, the octopus
is able to hold onto its food easily.

1. Why does an octopus sometimes become frightened?

_____

2. What happens when an octopus becomes frightened?

_____

3. What happens when an enemy attacks an octopus?

_____

4. What happens as a result of the suction cups on the octopus's arms?

_____

Solar Eclipse Safety

Read the passage. Then write an effect for each cause.

A solar eclipse occurs when the moon moves in front of the sun. Since the moon blocks most of the sunlight, people on Earth see only a small ring of light around the moon. A solar eclipse is an astonishing event. However, no one should ever look at an eclipse directly, through binoculars, or through a telescope. Why? The lens of your eye will focus the sun's light to a small spot on a membrane at the back of your eye called the retina, which can cause permanent eye damage—even blindness! Instead, look at the eclipse through a pinhole projector. A pinhole projector is simple to make. Go to an Internet search engine on a computer at home, school, or the library and enter "solar eclipse pinhole projector" for step-by-step directions.

Cause	Effect
1. The moon moves in front of the sun.	_____ _____
2. The moon blocks most of the sunlight.	_____ _____
3. A solar eclipse is an astonishing event.	_____ _____
4. A solar eclipse can cause permanent eye damage or blindness.	_____ _____
5. People make and use pinhole projectors.	_____ _____

 Unit 16 • Everyday Comprehension Intervention Activities Grade 5 • ©2010 Newmark Learning, LLC

The Western States

Read the passage. Then fill in the missing causes and effects.

Since America's western states are full of interesting attractions, people from all over the world plan vacations there. For example, people go to Cheyenne, Wyoming, every summer to see the world's largest rodeo. Hanauma Bay, Hawaii, attracts visitors who love beautiful beaches and sea animals. People visit Virginia City, Nevada, to see Comstock Lode, which once produced billions of dollars in gold and silver. They go to Bryce Canyon National Park in Utah to see rock formations called hoodoos, and they go to Sequoia National Park in California to see the largest trees in the world. A desert called Death Valley stretches across eastern California and western Nevada. The temperature can rise as high as 134°F (57°C). As a result, few people choose to visit in the summer. However, tourists flock to see the beautiful flowers that bloom in Death Valley after the spring rains.

1. **Cause:** America's western states are full of interesting attractions.
   Effect: _____

2. **Cause:** _____
   Effect: People visit Cheyenne, Wyoming, in the summer.

3. **Cause:** Many people love beautiful beaches and sea animals.
   Effect: _____

4. **Cause:** _____
   Effect: People visit Virginia City, Nevada.

5. **Cause:** People like to see unusual rock formations and large trees.
   Effect: _____

6. **Cause:** _____
   Effect: People prefer to visit after the spring rains instead.

Assessment

Read the passage. Then fill in the graphic organizers to show three of the cause-and-effect relationships.

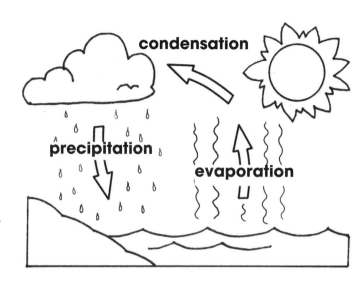

Water on Earth is always on the move. Picture a large body of water, such as a lake or ocean. The sun heats the water. As a result, the water becomes a vapor. This phase of the water cycle is called evaporation. During the next phase, condensation, the water vapor rises into the air and cools. Because the vapor cools, it changes back into a liquid state and forms clouds. Eventually, the clouds get heavy and cannot hold the water. This causes the water to fall to Earth as precipitation—rain, sleet, hail, or snow. Some of the precipitation falls directly into a body of water, and other parts make their way to the body of water as run-off. Either way, the water cycle continues!

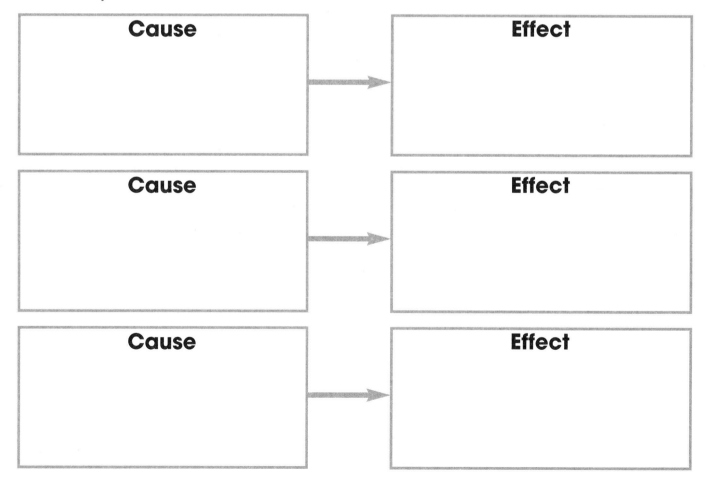

Cause		Effect
	→	

Cause		Effect
	→	

Cause		Effect
	→	

      Unit 16 • Everyday Comprehension Intervention Activities Grade 5 • ©2010 Newmark Learning, LLC

Overview Making Inferences in Fiction

Directions and Sample Answers for Activity Pages

Day 1	See "Provide a Real-World Example" below.
Day 2	Read and discuss the story. Then ask students to color the circles in front of the best answers. (**1:** Doris is frowning and has tight shoulders when she arrives. Doris asked Dr. Forester to check out Big Guy's injury. **2:** Many people frown and have tight shoulders when they are worried. **3:** Doris was worried about Big Guy, but now she is relieved.)
Day 3	Read and discuss the story. Then ask students to answer the questions. (**1:** Coyote kept complaining. The creek swelled around Coyote and tossed him out. **2:** Impatient people are easily upset by complainers. **3:** The creek is not patient.)
Day 4	Read and discuss the story. Then ask students to write their ideas in the boxes. (**Clues:** Lorianna is the best athlete in school. Mara reminds Lorianna that the track captain has to give the pep talk. **Already Know:** Kids often pick the best athlete as their team captain. **Inference:** Lorianna is the captain of the track team.)
Day 5	Read the story together. Ask students to record clues, prior knowledge, and an inference. Afterward, meet individually with students to discuss their results. Use their responses to plan further instruction and review. (**Clues:** Josh keeps giving Thomas excuses for not going for a boat ride. Thomas returns from the cabin with a sack. **Prior Knowledge:** People keep food and snacks in cabins. **Inference:** Thomas has something to eat in the sack.)

Provide a Real-World Example

◆ On cards, write scenarios for students to pantomime, such as *You just got a huge package in the mail* or *Your favorite cousin just called to say he won't be able to come to your soccer game.*

◆ Invite students to take turns acting out a scenario without speaking while classmates try to figure out what is happening. **Say:** *Use the actor's clues along with your own prior knowledge to figure out, or infer, what situation the actor is pantomiming.*

◆ After each pantomime, discuss students' inferences. **Ask:** *What clues did the actor give? What prior knowledge did you use to help make the inference?* Point out that an inference, while logical, may not always be correct.

◆ Hand out the Day 1 activity page. Then ask students to study the clues in the drawings on the page and use their prior knowledge to write an inference for each one. Allow time for students to share and compare their results.

◆ Explain that students can also make inferences when they read stories. Write the following on chart paper:

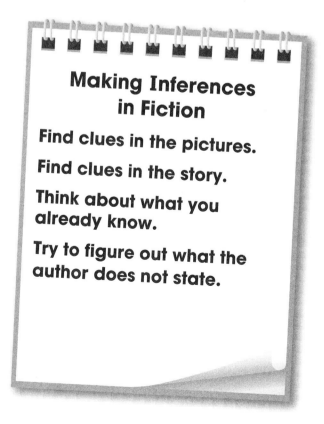

Making Inferences in Fiction

Find clues in the pictures.

Find clues in the story.

Think about what you already know.

Try to figure out what the author does not state.

What Are They Doing?

Look for clues in each picture. Then write an inference.

Inference

_____

_____

_____

Inference

_____

_____

_____

Big Guy

Read the story. Then read the questions and color the circles in front of the best answers.

Doris ran to Big Guy's stall and gave her horse a pat on the neck. "Good boy," she said softly. Then she looked at Dr. Forester. "Thank you for getting here so quickly," she said.

"I'm happy to help," said Dr. Forester. "What happened?"

"Big Guy did fine when I rode him today, but he skidded and fell when I was leading him back to his stall," said Doris. "I cleaned the scrape right away to get rid of the dirt and grass."

"Did you have any saline solution on hand?" the vet asked.

"Yes," Doris replied. "I also used some antibiotic cream and bandaged the wound."

"You did all the right things," said Dr. Forester. "He'll have some discomfort for a few days, but the injury isn't serious."

Doris relaxed her shoulders and smiled for the first time since she'd arrived at the horse's stall. "Thanks, Dr. Forester," she said.

1. Which clues are in the story?

○ Big Guy belongs to Dr. Forester.
○ Doris is frowning and has tight shoulders when she arrives.
○ Doris won't be able to ride Big Guy again for a long time.
○ Doris asked Dr. Forester to check out Big Guy's injury.

2. What do you already know?

○ Most veterinarians prefer to take care of horses.
○ People must always call a vet when their horses are injured.
○ Many people frown and have tight shoulders when they are worried.
○ Horses often skid and fall when they are going back to their stalls after riding.

3. Which is the best inference?

○ Dr. Forester is worried about Doris and Big Guy.
○ Dr. Forester will teach Doris how to take better care of Big Guy.
○ Doris wishes Dr. Forester would do more to help Big Guy.
○ Doris was worried about Big Guy, but now she is relieved.

Coyote's Complaints

Read the story. Then answer each question.

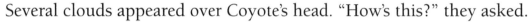

Coyote was out walking one hot afternoon. "I'm hot," Coyote said. "I want a cloud."

A cloud floated over Coyote to shade him. "How's this?" the cloud asked.

"I'm still hot," Coyote said, wiping sweat from his brow. "I want more clouds."

Several clouds appeared over Coyote's head. "How's this?" they asked.

"Still hot," Coyote complained. "I want rain."

The clouds rained on Coyote. "How's this?" they asked again.

"My feet are hot," Coyote said. "I want a creek."

A creek appeared, and Coyote splashed into it. "It needs to be deeper," he growled. Suddenly, the creek swelled around Coyote and tossed him out.

As Coyote lay on the bank, some buzzards arrived. "I wonder if he's dead," they remarked.

"No!" Coyote shouted. "Go away!"

1. What events are clues about how the creek feels?

_____

_____

2. What do you already know?

_____

_____

3. What inference can you make about the creek?

_____

_____

Rocket Woman

Read the story. Then write your ideas in the boxes.

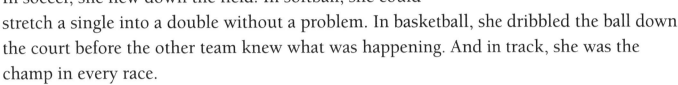

Everyone agreed that Lorianna was the best athlete in the school. Even the boys said she was talented—for a girl. But none of them dared to race her.

Lorianna loved all sports, especially the running part. In soccer, she flew down the field. In softball, she could stretch a single into a double without a problem. In basketball, she dribbled the ball down the court before the other team knew what was happening. And in track, she was the champ in every race.

One Monday, Lorianna got out of class a few minutes late. "You'd better hurry, Rocket Woman," yelled her friend Mara. "Today's the first day of track practice, and the captain has to give the pep talk!"

I know from the story that . . .

I already know . . .

I can infer that . . .

Assessment

Read the story. Then write the clues, your prior knowledge, and an inference in the boxes.

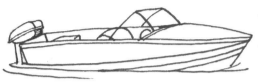

"Can we go out in the boat today? Please?" Thomas begged his big brother. "You promised we could go when the lake was calm."

"It's really hot today," replied Josh.

"No problem!" said Thomas. "I have sunscreen and a hat."

"Your life vest is hanging on a hook in the cabin," said Josh.

"No problem!" said Thomas. "I'll run and get it right now."

Thomas returned a few minutes later with his vest and a sack. "Can we go now?" he asked.

"You might get hungry," said Josh.

"No problem," Thomas said, holding up his sack.

Clues	Prior Knowledge

Inference

Overview Making Inferences in Nonfiction

Directions and Sample Answers for Activity Pages

Day 1	See "Provide a Real-World Example" below.
Day 2	Read and discuss the passage. Then ask students to color the circles in front of the best answers. (**1:** People had rules about stagecoach behavior. The book includes details about the history of public transportation. **2:** People often make rules in response to problems that occur. **3:** Stagecoach companies had to set rules because some travelers were rude.)
Day 3	Read and discuss the e-mail. Then ask students to complete the sentences. (**1:** e-mail, Ms. Townley. **2:** aisles. **3:** stores, aisles. **4:** manager, store.)
Day 4	Read and discuss the passage. Then ask students to write their ideas in the boxes. (**Evidence:** Young kids are not ready to use some of the tools and appliances that older kids use. **Already Know:** Many families have children of different ages. **Inference:** An adult should be present to make sure all the children are using age-appropriate tools and appliances when working in the kitchen.)
Day 5	Read the passage together. Ask students to record evidence, prior knowledge, and an inference. Afterward, meet individually with students to discuss their results. Use their responses to plan further instruction and review. (**Evidence:** The show has general admission seating. **Prior Knowledge:** General admission seating means no seats are reserved. People like to have good seats. **Inference:** People will get to the show early to try to get the best seats.)

Provide a Real-World Example

◆ Hand out the Day 1 activity page.

◆ **Say:** *Not long ago, I saw some kids walking into a skating rink. Some of them were carrying gifts. What do you think was going on?* Remind students that they can use evidence from the situation along with their own prior knowledge to figure out, or infer, what happened.

◆ Invite students to share their inferences. **Ask:** *What evidence did I give you? What prior knowledge did you use to help make the inference?* Remind them that an inference, while logical, may not always be correct.

◆ Ask students to study the evidence in the drawings and use their prior knowledge to write an inference for each one. Allow time for students to share and compare their results.

◆ Explain that students can also make inferences when they read. Write the following on chart paper:

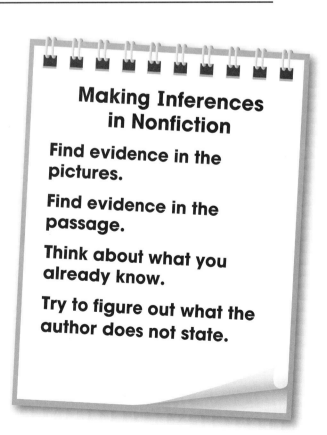

Making Inferences in Nonfiction

Find evidence in the pictures.

Find evidence in the passage.

Think about what you already know.

Try to figure out what the author does not state.

What's Going On?

Look for clues in each picture. Then write an inference.

Inference

_____

_____

_____

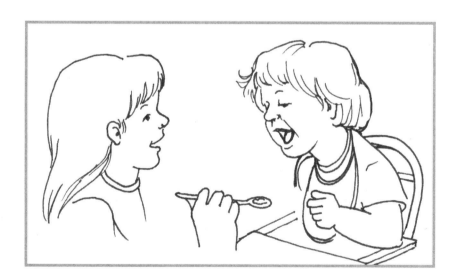

Inference

_____

_____

_____

Stagecoaches of the 1800s

Read the book review. Then read the questions and color the circles in front of the best answers.

Name of Book: *Stagecoaches of the 1800s*
Author: Butch James
Number of Pages: 108
Comments: I enjoyed reading this book. I learned a lot about the history of public transportation. The rules about stagecoach behavior were interesting and funny. Here are my favorites:

1. No smoking pipes or cigars if ladies are in the coach.
2. No rough language if ladies are present.
3. No loud snoring or napping on a fellow passenger's shoulder.
4. Avoid greasing hair because dust sticks to it.
5. Buffalo robes are supplied during cold weather. Hogging robes is not allowed. Anyone doing so will have to ride outside the coach with the driver.

1. Which pieces of evidence are in the passage?
○ People had rules about stagecoach behavior.
○ No one has ridden a stagecoach since the 1800s.
○ Most men smoked pipes or cigars while riding stagecoaches.
○ The book includes details about the history of public transportation.

2. What do you already know?
○ Buffalo robes are the warmest type of blanket.
○ People often make rules in response to problems that occur.
○ Few people nap or snore while riding public transportation today.
○ Most books about history are not as entertaining as this one appears to be.

3. Which is the best inference?
○ Rules from long ago were funny.
○ Rules from today will seem funny to people in the future.
○ Stagecoach companies had to set rules because some travelers were rude.
○ The same rules should apply to people who ride public transportation today.

Science Fair

Read the e-mail. Then complete each sentence.

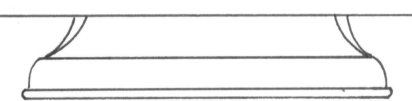

Dear Ms. Townley:

Hi! My name is Reggie. We're having a science fair at my school. I often see sturdy boxes sitting in your aisles. May I have four of them for my project? I'm going to make a home recycling center with containers for cans, bottles, paper, and plastic. I'll also have a computer presentation about all the recycling facilities in our community. My dad said he could pick up the boxes in his truck if it's okay with you. Please write back soon. Thank you!

Reggie McMillan

1. Reggie wrote an _____ message to _____.

2. Reggie had seen boxes sitting in her _____.

3. I know that _____ sometimes have boxes in the _____.

4. I can infer that Reggie is writing to the _____ of a _____.

Kids in the Kitchen

Read the passage. Then write your ideas in the boxes.

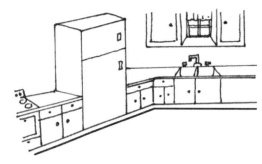

Most kids love to eat, so they love to help in the kitchen. However, safety is always a concern. The following are some general guidelines for using kitchen tools and appliances at different ages:

Ages 6 and under: blunt scissors for cutting soft foods, mixing spoons, whisk, non-electric egg beater, rolling pin, blunt butter knife or sandwich spreader, lemon squeezer, cookie and biscuit cutters, potato masher, and can opener

Ages 7–9: all of the above, plus blunt knife for cutting soft foods, cheese grater, and potato peeler

Ages 10–12: all of the above, plus sharper knives, blender, food processor, and microwave

---

I know from the passage that . . .

I already know . . .

I can infer that . . .

Assessment

Read the advertisement. Then write the evidence, your prior knowledge, and an inference in the boxes.

Cats Is Coming Soon!

A Purr-fect Musical!
Don't miss it!

Valley Players
Bleaker Hall
Saturday, March 23
Shows at 2 p.m. and 8 p.m.
General Admission Seating

Ticket Prices: Adults: $25

Children: $10 Seniors: $20

Box Office: 555-TICKETS

Evidence

Prior Knowledge

Inference

Overview Drawing Conclusions in Fiction

Directions and Sample Answers for Activity Pages

Day 1	See "Provide a Real-World Example" below.
Day 2	Read and discuss the story. Then ask students to circle the best conclusion and the clues that support it. (**Conclusion:** Alex knew he shouldn't be in the gym, so he didn't want anyone to see him. **Clues:** didn't see anybody; didn't want to turn on the light; quietly climbed to the last row of seats; looked around; slipped in; walked down a spooky hall.)
Day 3	Read and discuss the story. Then ask students to complete the sentences. (**1:** disappearing faster than they used to. **2:** squirrels, backyard. **3:** squirrel, the patio. **4:** animal tracks, the plate. **5:** squirrels are eating some of the seeds off the plate.)
Day 4	Read and discuss the story. Then ask students to color the circles in front of the best answers. (**1:** Heno, the god of thunder, lived in the falls. The god of thunder moved to the sky with his family. The maiden's canoe floated toward a thundering waterfall. Heno had a thundering voice. **2:** According to legend, the thundering echo is Heno's voice coming from the sky.)
Day 5	Read the story together. Ask students to write the story clues and a conclusion on their graphic organizers. Afterward, meet individually with students to discuss their results. Use their responses to plan further instruction and review. (**Clues:** peeping sound, tiny crack, holes in the shells, tip of a beak, science logs. **Conclusion:** The class has an incubator for hatching chicks as a science project.)

Provide a Real-World Example

◆ Hand out the Day 1 activity page.

◆ Give each student a card with three headings: *Equipment Needed, Number of Players,* and *Important Rule.* Ask students to fill in each category about a game they have played.

◆ Shuffle the cards. One at a time, invite students to choose a card and read the three clues aloud. **Say:** *Using several clues to figure something out is drawing a conclusion. Use the clues to draw a conclusion about the name of the game.* Once students have determined the game, ask the student who provided the clues to verify the conclusion.

◆ After all the students have had a turn, ask them to record the information from their chosen card onto their sheets.

◆ Explain that students can draw conclusions when they read stories. Write the following on chart paper:

Drawing Conclusions in Fiction

Find clues in pictures.

Find clues in the story.

Think about what makes sense based on the clues.

The Name of the Game

Use clues to draw conclusions.

Equipment Needed

+

Number of Players

+

Important Rule

=

Conclusion

The Mustangs

Read the story. Then draw a circle around the best conclusion and the clues that support it.

"Hey, Frankie," Alex called. "Guess what? I got to watch the Mustangs practice yesterday. Well, at least for a little while."

"No way!" said Frankie. "At the community college?"

"Uh-huh," Alex replied. "I walk right by the gym on my way home from school. The back door was open. I looked around and didn't see anybody, so I slipped in."

"Then what?" Frankie asked.

"It was dark, but I didn't want to turn on the light. I walked down a spooky hall and quietly climbed to the last row of seats. But after a few minutes, an assistant coach saw me and told me I had to leave."

"Can I try it with you after school today?" asked Frankie.

"No," said Alex. "The coach who walked me out said the door would be locked from now on."

Conclusion

Frankie is going to tell on Alex for sneaking into the community college gym.

Alex knew he shouldn't be in the gym, so he didn't want anyone to see him.

Alex and Frankie will ask the assistant coach if they can attend one of the Mustangs' practices.

Clues That Support the Conclusion

friends with Frankie	yesterday
community college	gym
back door was open	looked around
didn't see anybody	slipped in
didn't want to turn on the light	walked down a spooky hall
quietly climbed to the last row of seats	assistant coach
had to leave	door locked from now on

A Plate of Seeds

Read the story. Then complete each sentence.

Naomi put on her jacket and went out on the patio. She set a plate of seeds on the ground. When she came inside, she saw her sister. "I just put out more seeds for the birds," she said.

"That's good," Maureen said. "There isn't much for the birds to eat in the winter."

"I've been doing it for several days," Naomi remarked. "But the seeds seem to disappear a lot faster than they used to."

"Do squirrels eat seeds?" asked Maureen. "We have several that live in the trees in our backyard. I even saw one sunning itself on the patio yesterday."

"I don't know. I've never seen a squirrel at the plate," Naomi replied.

The next morning, the patio was covered with snow. When Naomi went out to check on the seeds, she saw animal tracks from the edge of the patio to the plate. "I'm going to look up those tracks in my nature book," she told Maureen.

1. **Naomi noticed that the seeds are** _____.

2. **Several** _____ **live in the trees in Naomi and Maureen's**

_____.

3. **Maureen saw a** _____ **sunning itself on**

_____.

4. **Naomi saw** _____ **by**

_____ **after a snow.**

5. **I can conclude that**

_____

_____.

The Maid of the Mist

Read the story. Then read the questions and color the circles in front of the best answers.

According to legend, a maiden once floated in a canoe toward a thundering waterfall. "Help!" she cried as her canoe swirled in the mist.

Heno, the god of thunder, lived in the falls. "I've got you," he said softly, trying not to frighten her with his thundering voice.

Heno cared for the maiden, and to his delight, she married his son. One day, the young woman learned that an evil snake was poisoning the water where her people lived. When Heno took her to warn them, the snake was furious. "I'll get Heno at the falls," it hissed. Heno hurled a lightning bolt at the approaching snake and killed it. However, the giant snake's body lodged in the river, forcing water into the falls and destroying Heno's home.

"We'll live in the clouds now," Heno thundered, gathering his family in the sky. And still today, there's a thundering echo in the falls.

1. Which clues are in the story?
○ Heno, the god of thunder, lived in the falls.
○ The god of thunder moved to the sky with his family.
○ Heno's son became the god of thunder.
○ The maiden's canoe floated toward a thundering waterfall.
○ The evil snake went over the falls when Heno's family left.
○ Heno had a thundering voice.

2. Which is the best conclusion?
○ According to legend, the maiden's people now live at the falls.
○ According to legend, the evil snake still hisses at the god of thunder.
○ According to legend, the thundering echo is Heno's voice coming from the sky.

Assessment

Read the story. Then write the story clues and a conclusion in the boxes.

Just as Ms. Emerson finished the day's read-aloud chapter, the students heard it. "Peep!"

They rushed to the table. "Look!" said Addison. "A tiny crack!"

"The bell will ring in five minutes," said Ms. Emerson. "Record your observations in your science log, and we'll look for any changes tomorrow."

The next morning, the class again gathered around the table. "I see holes in the shells," said Miranda.

"I see the tip of a beak!" said Carter.

"And there's another one!" said Nia.

"Grab your science logs again," said Ms. Emerson. "I have a feeling this is going to be an eventful morning!"

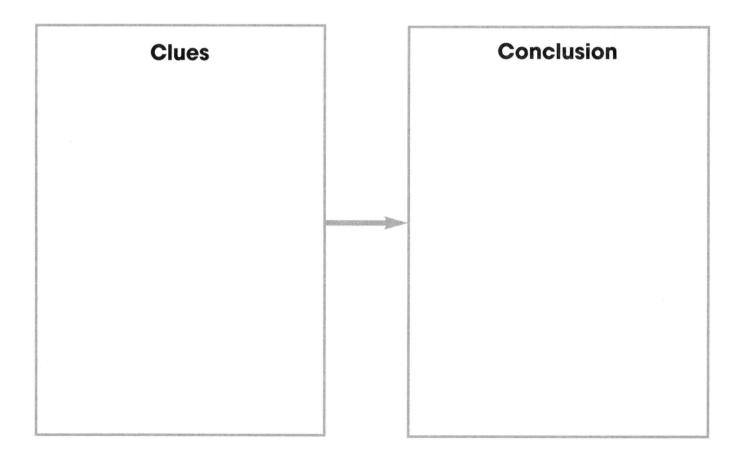

Clues	**Conclusion**

Overview Drawing Conclusions in Nonfiction

Directions and Sample Answers for Activity Pages

Day 1	See "Provide a Real-World Example" below.
Day 2	Read and discuss the passage. Then ask students to circle the best conclusion and the evidence that supports it. (**Conclusion:** Bats' bodies and behaviors help them survive in many different types of habitats. **Evidence:** have excellent hearing; can hold their food while they eat; see well in the dark; crowd together to stay warm while they sleep; live in many places in the world; use their voices and ears instead of their eyes at night; fly and catch insects in the air; migrate to warmer climates or hibernate in winter.)
Day 3	Read and discuss the passage. Then ask students to answer the questions. (**1:** The weather was snowy and cold with freezing rain. **2:** He had a hard time seeing out the front window. **3:** He opened the other windows. Every few minutes, he stopped, got out, and cleared off the ice and snow. **4:** She thought there had to be a better, safer way to keep the window clean. She designed a device with a swinging arm and rubber blade. **5:** She invented the first windshield wiper.)
Day 4	Read and discuss the passage. Then ask students to color the circles in front of the best answers. (**1:** Drivers' attention is on their conversations rather than the road. They miss seeing unexpected changes in traffic. Speaking and listening interfere with awareness. Texters take their eyes off the road. Their ability to react is slowed. Some laws prohibit texting and/or talking on cell phones when driving. People are seriously distracted when using a cell phone while driving. **2:** Using a cell phone while driving is dangerous.)
Day 5	Read the passage together. Ask students to write the evidence and a conclusion on their graphic organizers. Afterward, meet individually with students to discuss their results. Use their responses to plan further instruction and review. (**Evidence:** Two-thirds of house fires occur in buildings with no smoke alarms. The majority of injuries and deaths in house fires are caused by breathing smoke and dangerous gases. These silent intruders can move through a house unnoticed. Several states have laws requiring that smoke alarms be installed in all homes. A firefighter or inspector must check that smoke alarms are working. **Conclusion:** Working smoke alarms can save people's lives.)

Provide a Real-World Example

◆ Hand out the Day 1 activity page.

◆ **Say:** *I recently drove by a park. I saw grown-ups and kids in green T-shirts. Each one had on gloves and was carrying a trash bag. I saw the recycling truck nearby, too.* Remind students that using several clues to figure something out is drawing a conclusion. **Ask:** *What conclusion can you draw from this situation?*

◆ Invite students to share their conclusions. **Ask:** *What evidence did you use to draw your conclusion?*

◆ Ask students to study the evidence in the drawings and write a conclusion for each set. Allow time for students to share and compare their results.

◆ Explain that students can also draw conclusions when they read. Write the following on chart paper:

Drawing Conclusions in Nonfiction

Find evidence in pictures.

Find evidence in the text.

Think about what makes sense based on the evidence.

Volunteers

Look at the clues in each column. Then write or draw your conclusion in the box below.

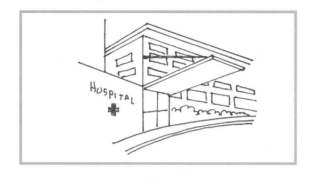

+

+

=

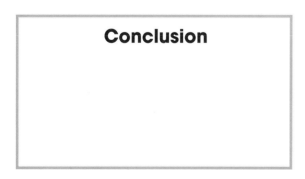

Conclusion

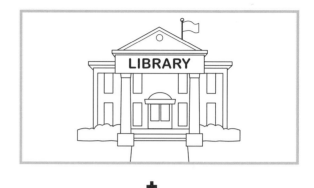

+

+

=

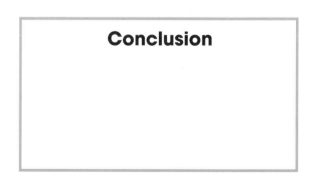

Conclusion

Bat Facts

Read the passage. Then draw a circle around the best conclusion and the evidence that supports it.

Bats live in many places around the world. Bats that live in cool climates migrate to warmer climates or hibernate in the winter. Those that hibernate have learned to crowd together to stay warm while they sleep. Bats hunt for food at night. Since they don't see well in the dark, they make little squeaks and listen for an echo to determine if an object is nearby. They have big ears and excellent hearing. Bats have remarkable wings, too. Besides allowing them to fly and catch insects in the air, their wings serve as hands. With a "thumb" and four "fingers" on each wing, bats can hold their food while they eat.

Conclusion

Bats would have a better chance of survival if they could see well in the dark.

Bats' bodies and behaviors help them survive in many different types of habitats.

Bats that live in warm climates are more likely to survive than those that live in colder climates.

Evidence That Supports the Conclusion

have excellent hearing

can hold their food while they eat

migrate to colder climates or hibernate in summer

see well in the dark

have remarkable hands

crowd together to stay warm while they sleep

live in many places in the world

use their voices and ears instead of their eyes at night

stay away from other bats that might harm them

stay near familiar objects

fly and catch insects in the air

migrate to warmer climates or hibernate in winter

A Slow, Snowy Ride

Read the passage. Then answer each question.

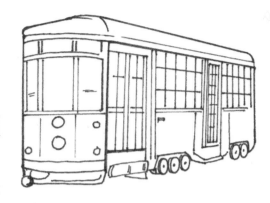

Over a hundred years ago, a woman named Mary Anderson went on a trip to New York City. It was wintertime, and the weather was snowy and cold with freezing rain. She got on a streetcar and noticed that the driver was having a hard time seeing out the front window. He had the other windows open to help him watch where he was going. Still, every few minutes he had to stop the streetcar, get out, and clear off the ice and snow. "There has to be a better, safer way to keep the window clean," thought Mary. When she got back home, she designed a device with a swinging arm and rubber blade.

1. What were the weather conditions the day Mary Anderson rode the streetcar?

_____

2. What problem did the driver experience?

_____

3. What steps did the driver take to solve the problem?

_____

4. What was Mary's reaction to the problem and the driver's solutions?

_____

5. What can you conclude about Mary Anderson?

_____

Cell Phone Safety

**Read the passage. Then read the questions
and color the circles in front of the best answers.**

Talking on a cell phone while driving has become an important research topic. Scientists and law-enforcement officials are studying how drivers are affected by this activity. Some results show that drivers are seriously distracted when using a cell phone while driving. Their attention is on the conversation rather than on the road, as both speaking and listening interfere with awareness of the immediate environment. Drivers miss seeing unexpected, even life-threatening changes in traffic, and their ability to react is slowed because they're usually driving with one hand. An even greater problem is texting while driving, as this involves taking their eyes off the road. Many cities and states are currently passing laws prohibiting texting, talking on cell phones, or both while driving.

1. Which pieces of evidence are in the passage?

○ Drivers' attention is on their conversations rather than the road.

○ They miss seeing unexpected changes in traffic.

○ Scientists and law-enforcement officials use cell phones while driving.

○ Speaking and listening interfere with awareness.

○ Texters take their eyes off the road.

○ Their ability to react is slowed.

○ Some laws prohibit texting and/or talking on cell phones when driving.

○ The immediate environment is less important than conversations.

○ People are seriously distracted when using a cell phone while driving.

2. Which is the best conclusion?

○ Cell-phone reception is bad in cars.

○ Drivers do not like cell phones.

○ Using a cell phone while driving is dangerous.

Assessment

**Read the passage. Then write the evidence and
a conclusion in the boxes.**

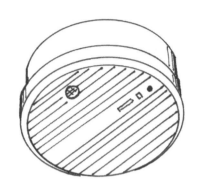

Many homes today have smoke alarms. But according
to recent studies, two-thirds of house fires occur in
buildings with no smoke alarms. In other structures, the
alarms don't work because people have forgotten to test
them and check the batteries. The majority of injuries and deaths in house fires are
caused by breathing smoke and dangerous gases. Without smoke alarms, these silent
intruders can move through a house unnoticed, especially when everyone is asleep.
Several states have laws requiring that smoke alarms be installed in all homes. Before
someone can sell a house, a firefighter or inspector must check that its smoke alarms
are working.

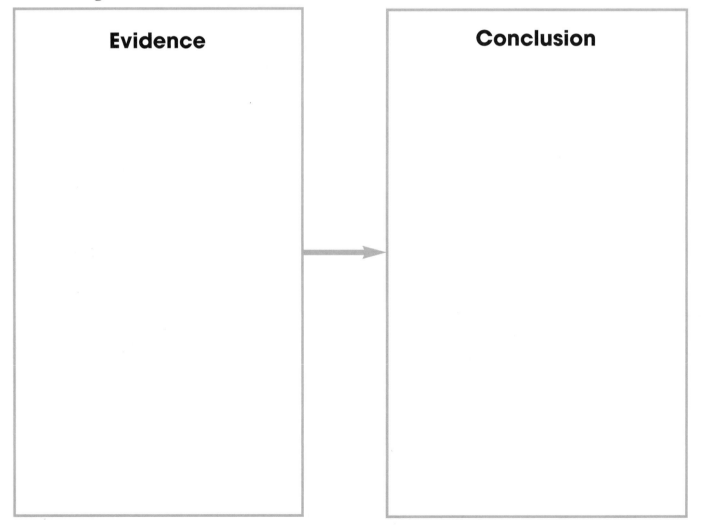

Evidence	Conclusion

Overview Evaluating Author's Purpose in Fiction

Directions and Sample Answers for Activity Pages

Day 1	See "Provide a Real-World Example" below.
Day 2	Read and discuss the story. Then ask students to color the circles in front of the best answers. (**1:** Frederick tells a joke about ponds. Frederick says Marta stole his joke. Marta complains about Frederick's jokes. Marta tells a joke about sea monsters. Frederick tells a joke about sharks. **2:** to entertain readers with a story about jokes.)
Day 3	Read and discuss the story. Then ask students to complete the clues and write the author's purpose. (**1:** talk. **2:** talk. **3:** blue feathers. **4:** a blue coat. **5:** lake, four days. **6:** advice. **7:** birds, coyote. **Author's Purpose:** The author wants to entertain readers with a pourquoi tale that explains something in nature.)
Day 4	Read and discuss the story. Then ask students to answer the questions. (**1:** A man talked for several hours. A man talked for several days. Every man in the state came to tell his story. The contest lasted for years. **2:** I'm all out of lies. I trained a bear to make my supper. I climbed the tallest mountain in the world with just a clothesline rope. I've never told a lie in my life. **3:** The author wanted to entertain readers with a tall tale that has funny details and exaggeration.)
Day 5	Read the story together. Ask students to record clues and an author's purpose on their graphic organizers. Afterward, meet individually with students to discuss their results. Use their responses to plan further instruction and review. (**Clues:** innkeepers were gone; left hundred-dollar bill on the counter; inn was destroyed by a storm years ago; in ruins; broken front door; remains of the front counter; the hundred-dollar bill. **Author's Purpose:** The author wants to entertain readers with a spooky story.)

Provide a Real-World Example

- ◆ Hand out the Day 1 activity page.

- ◆ **Say:** *The pictures on this page are examples of hink pinks. A hink pink is a one-syllable adjective and one-syllable noun that rhyme. For example, the first picture shows a fat cat. Ask students to write* **fat cat** *on the lines. Then* **say:** *People can entertain each other by thinking of hink pinks.*

- ◆ Invite students to figure out the rest of the hink pinks. (big pig, hen pen, frail quail) Then allow time for them to share their ideas with the group.

- ◆ **Say:** *Authors often write to entertain, too. We can look for clues to help evaluate the author's purpose when we read.* Write the following on chart paper:

Evaluating Author's Purpose in Fiction

Find clues in the pictures.

Find clues in the story. Think like the author.

Think about how the author tries to entertain.

Animal Hink Pinks

Look at each picture. Then write a hink pink for each picture.

_____

_____

_____

_____

Fishing with Frederick

Read the story. Then read the questions and color the cicles in front of the best answers.

"Your cousin Frederick is coming fishing with us today," said Dad.

"Oh, no!" said Marta. "I like him, but his jokes drive me crazy!"

"Did you say jokes?" asked Frederick as he burst through the door. "I know lots of fish jokes. Why do sharks only swim in salt water? Because pepper water makes them sneeze! Ha!"

Dad smiled. "Let's head for the pond," he said.

"What kind of rocks are always in ponds?" asked Frederick. "Wet ones! Ha!"

"What do sea monsters eat?" asked Marta as she opened the door. Dad and Frederick both stared at her. "Fish and ships! Ha!" she replied.

"You stole my next joke," Frederick complained.

1. Which are clues about why the author wrote this story?

○ Dad is ready to head for the pond.

○ Frederick tells a joke about ponds.

○ Frederick says Marta stole his joke.

○ Marta complains about Frederick's jokes.

○ Marta and Frederick are cousins.

○ Marta tells a joke about sea monsters.

○ Dad, Marta, and Frederick are going fishing.

○ Frederick tells a joke about sharks.

2. Which is the author's main purpose?

○ to inform readers about fishing

○ to entertain readers with a story about telling jokes

○ to persuade readers to learn lots of jokes

How Bluebirds and Coyotes Got Their Colors

Read the story. Look for funny, unusual, or surprising details. Then complete the clues and write the author's purpose.

Two birds were flying over a lake. "Look at how blue the lake is!" chirped the first bird.

"Let's bathe in it," suggested the second bird. "Maybe our feathers will turn blue."

"Yes, let's!" said the first bird, diving into the water. The birds stayed at the lake for four days. Soon their dull feathers fell out and they had beautiful, blue feathers.

Coyote came along. "I've never seen blue birds before. I want to be blue, too," he said.

"You must bathe in the blue lake for four days," the birds advised.

Coyote went to the lake. "I'm not waiting four days," he said. Instead, he bathed four times. "Hey, I'm blue!" he cried. He admired his coat all the way home. But suddenly he slipped and fell in the dirt.

And that is why, today, bluebirds are blue and coyotes are the color of dirt.

Clues

1. The birds can _____.
2. The coyote can _____.
3. The birds wanted _____.
4. The coyote wanted _____.
5. The birds stayed at the _____ for _____.
6. The coyote decided not to follow the birds' _____.
7. The _____ got what they wanted, but the _____ did not.

Author's Purpose

_____

_____

The Contest

Read the story. Then answer the questions.

Myer the Liar held a contest. "I'm all out of lies," he announced. "I'll give a hound dog to the man who tells the biggest fib."

"I'm sure to win," one man exclaimed. He talked for several hours. "And that's how I trained a bear to make my supper," he finished.

"That's quite a story," said another man. "But I have a better one." He talked for several days. "And that's how I climbed the tallest mountain in the world with just a clothesline rope," he concluded.

Every man in the state came to tell his story. The contest lasted for years. Finally, the last man stood up. "I'm sorry, but I have no story to tell. You see, I've never told a lie in my life."

"Congratulations!" said Myer. "You win the hound!"

1. What lies did the storyteller tell?

_____

_____

2. What lies did the characters in the story tell?

_____

_____

3. Why do you think the author wrote this story?

_____

_____

Assessment

Read the story. Then write the clues and author's purpose in the boxes.

A family was traveling when it began to rain. Soon, they couldn't see the road in front of them. "There's an inn. Let's stop for the night," suggested the mother.

A kind-looking couple greeted the family at the door. "Welcome," the man said. The innkeepers showed them to their cozy room. When they awoke the next morning, the sun was shining. They packed their bags and went to the front desk, but the innkeepers were gone. So the family left a hundred-dollar bill on the counter and left.

At a nearby restaurant, the family told the owner about their fine night at the inn. "But that's not possible," the owner exclaimed. "That inn was destroyed by a storm years ago."

The family went back to the inn. "It's in ruins!" they exclaimed. Stepping through the broken front door, the children screamed, "Look!" There on the remains of the front counter was the hundred-dollar bill.

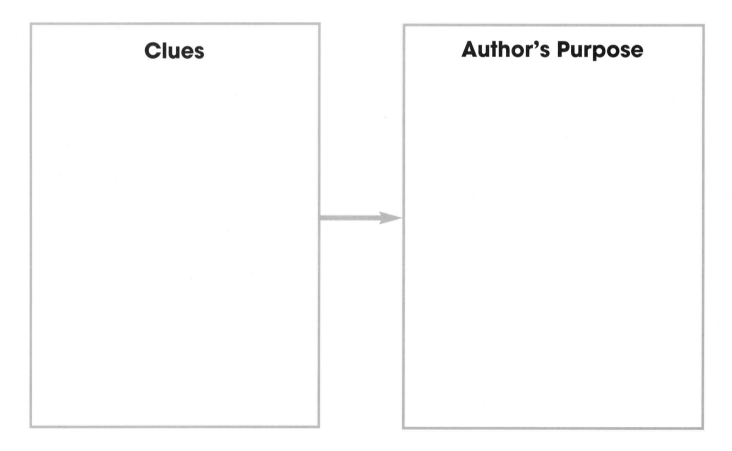

Clues

Author's Purpose

Overview Evaluating Author's Purpose in Nonfiction

Directions and Sample Answers for Activity Pages

Day 1	See "Provide a Real-World Example" below.
Day 2	Read and discuss the passage. Then ask students to color the circles in front of the best answers. (**1:** guide nature walks, studied forestry, present programs, keep people safe, like working outdoors, a park ranger, appreciate nature, keep animals safe. **2:** to inform readers about a park ranger's job.)
Day 3	Read and discuss the letter. Then ask students to answer the questions. (**1:** Mark wants to persuade his cousin Zak to come for a visit. **2:** haven't seen you in a long time; tons of fun things to do; camping at Noisy Pond; hilarious shows; really like the one coming up next; band concerts are amazing; best cook ever; perfect meal; sumptuous suppers; sleeping bags are ready.)
Day 4	Read and discuss the passage. Then ask students to draw a picture to go with the passage and write the author's purpose. (**Drawing:** Responses will vary, but may include a trunk of special quilts; china wrapped in quilts; quilts used for bedding; a folded quilt used as padding for the driver's seat; quilts covering cracks in a wagon; and quilts on the side of a wagon for protection. **Author's Purpose:** The author wants to inform readers about ways pioneer families used quilts.)
Day 5	Read the advertisement together. Ask students to record evidence and an author's purpose on their graphic organizers. Afterward, meet individually with students to discuss their results. Use their responses to plan further instruction and review. (**Evidence:** special ice cream; something new; rich; crunchy; fruity; better than apple pie; guests will rave; available at both stores; flying off the shelves. **Author's Purpose:** The author wants to persuade readers to buy Fried Apple Delight ice cream.)

Provide a Real-World Example

◆ Hand out the Day 1 activity page.

◆ **Say:** *My friend brought over a book for me to read. I wasn't sure I wanted to read it. He said the book is a genre I really like—historical fiction. He also said the book is on the store's best-seller list. Why do you think my friend said these things? What was he trying to do?*

◆ Discuss the ways your friend tried to persuade you to read the book. Then ask students to complete the sentences by the picture of the book.

◆ Ask students to write the title of a book they like and write two things they would say to try to persuade others to read it. Allow time for students to share their responses.

◆ **Say:** *Sometimes authors write nonfiction to persuade. Other times, they write nonfiction to inform. We can look for evidence to help us evaluate the author's purpose when we read.* Write the following on chart paper:

Evaluating Author's Purpose in Nonfiction

Find evidence in the pictures.

Find evidence in the text. Think like the author.

Think about how the author tries to persuade or inform.

Recommended Reading

Listen. Then complete each sentence.

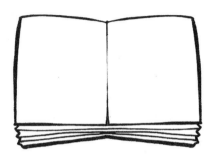

The book is a _____ you really like.

The book is on the store's _____ list.

Choose a book that you like. Then write two sentences that you think will make other people want to read this book.

My Book Title:

_____

1. _____

   _____

2. _____

   _____

Park Rangers

Read the passage. Then read the questions and color the circles in front of the best answers.

Have you thought about what you would like to do when you grow up? If you like working outdoors and appreciate nature, you might like to be a park ranger. Many park rangers have studied forestry, biology, or geology. Some park rangers work only in the summer, while others work all year. Part of a park ranger's job is to keep the animals that live in the park and the people who visit the park safe. For example, several rangers may have to move a bear to another part of the park if it's too close to visitors. Other jobs of a park ranger are guiding nature walks and presenting programs about the park and its wildlife. Next time you visit a large park, talk to the park ranger. The ranger can tell you even more about the job.

1. Which phrases are evidence that helps you figure out the author's purpose?
- ○ guide nature walks
- ○ might like
- ○ studied forestry
- ○ present programs
- ○ keep people safe
- ○ have you thought
- ○ like working outdoors
- ○ grow up
- ○ a park ranger
- ○ appreciate nature
- ○ visit a large park
- ○ keep animals safe

2. Which is the author's main purpose?
- ○ to entertain readers with a story about a bear
- ○ to persuade readers to become park rangers
- ○ to inform readers about a park ranger's job

Dear Zak

Read the letter. Then answer each question.

Dear Zak,

   Will you come for a visit? I haven't seen you in a long time. There are tons of fun things to do here. Dad said he'd take us camping at Noisy Pond. You should hear all the bullfrogs croaking this time of year! The community theater is doing some hilarious shows. I think you'd really like the one coming up next called *Please Step on the Grass*. We also have entertainment on the town square on Friday nights. The band concerts are amazing. And my mom is the best cook ever. You haven't eaten a perfect meal until you've had one of her sumptuous suppers. Please ask your parents tonight, and then give me a call. My sleeping bags are ready!

   Your cousin,
   Mark

1. What is Mark's main purpose in writing this letter?

_____

2. What phrases does Mark use in the letter to support this purpose?

_____

_____

_____

_____

Colonial Quilts

Read the passage. Draw a picture to go with the passage. Then write the author's purpose.

In preparation for the journey to western territories, pioneer women spent much of their time sewing and quilting. When they packed for the trip, they put the quilts that were most special to them in trunks and used other special quilts to wrap valued china. Then, they laid out their more ordinary quilts to use for bedding during the long wagon ride. Once the difficult journey began, the women found other uses for the quilts. They folded them to make padding for the driver's seat as the wagon jolted along the rocky, rutted trail. They covered cracks in the wagon with quilts to keep out the suffocating dust. They even used the quilts on the sides of the wagon for protection against attacks.

Author's Purpose

_____

_____

Assessment

Read the advertisement. Then write the evidence and author's purpose in the boxes.

**Need some special ice cream for a party?
In the mood for something new?**

Try Dreamy Creamy's Fried Apple Delight.
   It's rich—cinnamon and caramel!
   It's crunchy—candied walnuts!
   It's fruity—fried, buttery apple chunks!
   It's better than apple pie—your guests will rave!
   Available at both Dreamy Creamy stores.
   Buy now! It's flying off the shelves!

Evidence	Author's Purpose

Unit 22 • Everyday Comprehension Intervention Activities Grade 5 • ©2010 Newmark Learning, LLC

Overview Analyzing Text Structure and Organization in Fiction

Directions and Sample Answers for Activity Pages

Day 1	See "Provide a Real-World Example" below.
Day 2	Read and discuss the story. Then ask students to circle the two main text structures the author uses. (Sequence of Events, Problem and Solution.)
Day 3	Read and discuss the story. Then ask students to follow the directions and complete the sentences. (**1:** Compare and Contrast. **2:** Description, play the games.)
Day 4	Read and discuss the story. Then ask students to complete the sentences. (**1:** she got many compliments. **2:** he was envious of Ladybug. **3:** he crawled to a house where some children lived. **4:** she could see his spots. **5:** it had rained. **6:** the water washed off his spots. **7:** Cause and Effect.)
Day 5	Read the story together. Ask students to record clues about the main text structure on their graphic organizers. Afterward, meet individually with students to discuss their results. Use their responses to plan further instruction and review. (**Clues:** spicy smell of apple pie; aroma of baking bread; exquisitely decorated cakes; smooth and buttery; gooey; pans clanging; timers beeping; door opening and closing; customers "ooh-ing" and "ahh-ing." **Text Structure:** Description.)

Provide a Real-World Example

◆ Hand out the Day 1 activity page.

◆ **Say:** *Once I went to a music festival. It was amazing! I couldn't wait to e-mail my friends and family. I told them what I saw. I told them what I heard. I told them how it felt to sit at all the different stages. I even told them how the food from the food stands smelled and tasted. From these clues, my family and friends knew I was describing my experience.*

◆ Ask students to read the description of the music festival on their page. Then ask them to draw a picture based on the description. Allow time for students to compare drawings with their classmates.

◆ **Say:** *Description is one type of text structure we find when we read stories. We also find four other text structures.* Write the following on chart paper:

Analyzing Text Structure and Organization in Fiction

Look for words that describe.

Look for words that compare and contrast.

Look for words that tell about cause and effect.

Look for words that tell about a sequence of events.

Look for words that tell about a problem and a solution.

Music Festival

Read the passage. Then draw a picture based on the description you read.

I'm at the music festival. People are everywhere—great-grandparents, babies, and everyone in between. I can hear all types of music coming from the different stages. For some shows, I sit on hard bleachers. For others, I sit in my portable camping chair or on the soft grass. Heavenly food smells waft over the entire park. I'm trying lots of new treats. My favorite so far is grilled chicken on a stick, coated with a tangy sauce, and rolled in sesame seeds. I hope you can all come next year!

How the Buffalo Were Released on Earth

Read the story. Think about the clues. Then draw a circle around the two main text structures the author uses.

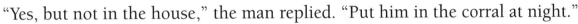

There were no buffalo on the prairie, and the native people were hungry. "I saw a herd of buffalo in a man's corral," said Coyote. "I'll get them for you."

That afternoon, Coyote went to the corral and changed himself into a dog. Soon, the man's son saw him. "Look, Father—a dog! Can I keep him?"

"Yes, but not in the house," the man replied. "Put him in the corral at night."

The boy played with his new pet the rest of the day. Coyote went for walks, fetched sticks, and wrestled in the grass. Finally, the tired boy put him in the corral and said good night.

As soon as the lights went out in the house, the dog opened the gate and chased the buffalo onto the prairie toward their new home. Then he returned to the village as Coyote—just in time for a celebration in his honor.

Text Structures:

Description

Sequence of Events

Compare and Contrast

Cause and Effect

Problem and Solution

Egg Games

**Read the story. Then follow the directions
and complete the sentences.**

Rich and Flo were ready to play Egg Toss. "I'm glad we wore old clothes," Flo said. "I ran too fast in the Egg-in-a-Spoon game, and my egg fell and broke. Raw egg splattered on my sneakers and jeans—yuck!"

"But the Egg Toss game won't be a race," Rich said.

"Still, the eggs will be raw," Flo reminded Rich. "Both games are definitely for outdoors."

Rich agreed. "I can think of two other ways Egg Toss is different from Egg-in-a-Spoon. We'll be partners, and we won't use spoons. Instead, we'll use our hands to catch and throw an egg."

"No problem," Flo said, laughing. "I don't want any more egg on me, so I hope to be the best egg catcher of all!"

1. Draw a line under the words **but, still, both, different,** and **instead**.

   These are signal words for the _____ text structure.

2. The author also uses the _____text structure
   to tell how to _____.

Black Beetle and Ladybug

Read the story. Then complete the sentences.

Black Beetle saw Ladybug. "Your spots are quite beautiful," he said.

"Thank you! I do get many compliments," Ladybug admitted.

Soon, envy overtook Black Beetle, so he decided to give himself spots. He crawled to a house where some children lived so he could borrow a stick of their red chalk. Black Beetle took the chalk home and drew big red spots on himself. Then he called Ladybug. "May I come over?" he asked.

"Certainly," Ladybug replied.

Since it had rained, Black Beetle had to go through puddles on the way. The last puddle was the deepest of all. "Oh, no!" he cried. "The water washed off every spot!" He did a quick about-face and started back home.

But Ladybug had already seen him. "How shiny you look after your bath, Black Beetle! Do come in for cookies and tea."

1. Insects thought Ladybug's spots were beautiful. As a result, _____
_____.

2. Black Beetle decided to give himself spots, because _____
_____.

3. Black Beetle needed a stick of red chalk. Consequently, _____
_____.

4. Black Beetle wanted to go to Ladybug's house so that _____
_____.

5. Black Beetle had to go through puddles on the way, because _____
_____.

6. Since Black Beetle went through puddles, _____
_____.

7. Based on these clues, the text structure for this story is _____
_____.

Assessment

Read the story. Then write clues about the main text structure on the graphic organizer.

"I love helping out at my uncle's bakery," David told Martina. "I think I like the spicy smell of apple pie in the oven best, although the aroma of baking bread makes me want to eat a whole loaf!"

Martina laughed. "I think his decorated cakes are exquisite. I saw a round cake with lilac frosting and burgundy flowers. It had lemon gumdrops in the centers of the flowers."

"Believe or not, those cakes taste even better than they look," said David. "I had a slice of chocolate cheesecake yesterday. It tasted like fudge—smooth and buttery."

"My favorite is the brownies," Martina said. "They're gooey, but sticky fingers are worth it."

"I even like the sounds of the bakery," said David. "Pans clanging, timers beeping, the door opening and closing . . ."

" . . . and the customers 'ooh-ing' and 'ahh-ing' as they check out the display cases," Martina added.

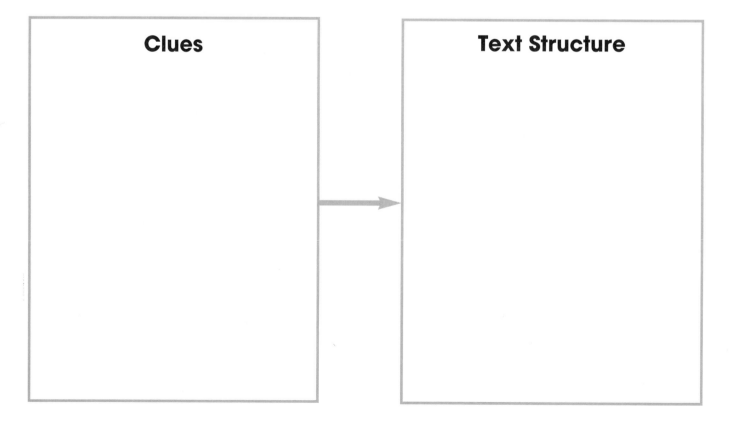

Clues	**Text Structure**

Unit 23 • Everyday Comprehension Intervention Activities Grade 5 • ©2010 Newmark Learning, LLC

Overview Analyzing Text Structure and Organization in Nonfiction

Directions and Sample Answers for Activity Pages

Day 1	See "Provide a Real-World Example" below.
Day 2	Read and discuss the passage. Then ask students to circle the two main text structures the author uses. (Sequence of Events, Problem and Solution.)
Day 3	Read and discuss the passage. Then ask students to follow the directions and complete the sentences. (**1:** Cause and Effect. **2:** Description, look like.)
Day 4	Read and discuss the passage. Then ask students to answer the questions. (**1:** usually come on gradually, stuffy or runny nose, sneezing, hacking cough, sore throat. **2:** usually come on quickly, fever, chills, fatigue, dry cough, body aches. **3:** respiratory illness, caused by viruses, chest discomfort, headaches. **4:** Compare and Contrast.)
Day 5	Read and discuss the passage. Ask students to record information about the main text structure on their graphic organizers. Afterward, meet individually with students to discuss their results. Use their responses to plan further instruction and review. (**Evidence:** strong, colorful nouns, verbs, adjectives, and adverbs, such as *leap, plunging, shocking, puffing out, troubleshooters, grueling, toil, blistering, choking, desperately, raging monster, searing, loom, innocent-looking, soaring, orange fingers, grasping, grimy, tough.* **Text Structure:** Description.)

Provide a Real-World Example

◆ Hand out the Day 1 activity page.

◆ **Say:** *I recently read directions for a math game. First, write addition problems on cards. Then, write the sums on the backs. Next, hold up the answer side while your classmates try to guess the problem. If someone guesses, hand that person the card. Finally, count how many cards everyone has. The one with the most cards is the winner!*

◆ Point out that the text had signal words, such as **first, then, next,** and **finally. Say:** *From this evidence, I knew the text structure was a sequence of events. In a how-to text, we also call this text structure steps in a process.*

◆ Ask students to cut out the blank cards and then follow the game directions in groups of three or four. Repeat the directions if needed.

◆ **Say:** *Sequence of events is one type of text structure we find when we read. We also find four other text structures.* Write the following on chart paper:

> **Analyzing Text Structure and Organization in Nonfiction**
>
> Look for words that describe.
>
> Look for words that compare and contrast.
>
> Look for words that tell about cause and effect.
>
> Look for words that tell about a sequence of events.
>
> Look for words that tell about a problem and a solution.

Sums

**Listen. Then cut out each card and create your own math game.
Draw addition problems on one side and sums on the other.**

Unit 24 • Everyday Comprehension Intervention Activities Grade 5 • ©2010 Newmark Learning, LLC

Salamander Crossing

Read the passage. Think about the evidence. Then draw a circle around the two main text structures the author uses.

The habitat for hundreds of spotted salamanders in Amherst, Massachusetts, is a hillside on Henry Street. However, the salamanders cross Henry Street each spring to lay their eggs in the small ponds on the other side. Because Henry Street is a busy road, and the salamanders cross in the dark, the journey is dangerous. Concerned environmentalists and citizens wanted to protect the salamanders from

motorists. So, in 1987, the town built tunnels under the street to provide a safe crossing for Henry Street's amphibians. Then, they had a contest to see who could design the best "salamander crossing" sign. The winner was a student from a local elementary school!

Text Structures:

Description

Sequence of Events

Compare and Contrast

Cause and Effect

Problem and Solution

Walking Sticks

Read the passage. Then follow the directions and complete the sentences.

Have you ever seen a long, thin insect that looks like a twig? It doesn't fly, but it walks slowly. Therefore, it's called a walking stick. Since it looks like part of a plant, it blends into its environment, making it difficult to see. The eggs of this insect look like seeds, so they are also hard to spot. Because a walking stick is easy to keep, some science teachers use it to teach their students about insects and nature. However, they know the importance of never releasing a walking stick into the wild if it's not native to the area. For example, a walking stick from India was once released in California. This species multiplies rapidly. As a result, hordes of hungry Indian walking sticks were soon devouring plants.

1. Draw a line under the words **therefore**, **since**, **so**, **because**, and **as a result**. These are signal words for the _____ text structure.

2. The author also uses the _____text structure to show what walking sticks and their eggs _____.

Cold or Flu?

Read the passage. Then answer the questions.

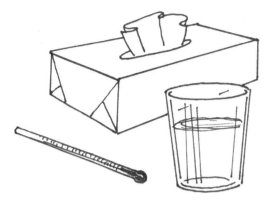

Many of us fall ill at least once in the winter.
Sometimes we get colds, and other times we get the
flu. How can we tell the difference? A cold and the
flu are both respiratory illnesses caused by viruses.
However, colds usually come on gradually, while flu
symptoms come on more quickly. The flu causes a fever, chills, fatigue, a dry cough, and
body aches. People with colds usually don't have fevers and body aches, but they do have
a stuffy or runny nose, a hacking cough, and they sneeze. Cold victims are more likely to
have a sore throat than people with the flu. Colds and the flu can cause chest discomfort
and headaches, but these symptoms are more common with the flu.

1. Which details describe colds?

_____

_____

2. Which details describe the flu?

_____

_____

3. What do colds and the flu have in common?

_____

_____

4. Based on this evidence, the text structure for this passage is

_____

_____ .

Name _____

Assessment

**Read the passage. Then write evidence about
the main text structure on the graphic organizer.**

The fastest way for firefighters to reach a forest
fire is by air. Smoke jumpers are firefighters who
leap from airplanes, plunging to the fire scene
below. Landing with a shocking thud, parachutes
puffing out above them, these troubleshooters are ready for the grueling work before
them. They toil in blistering heat and choking smoke day and night. Smoke jumpers dig
fire lines, trying desperately to control the raging monster. Searing flames can suddenly
loom from an innocent-looking bush, soaring upward like orange fingers grasping for the
sky. When a fire is finally under control, smoke jumpers continue their grimy work and
check for sparks. Smoke jumpers perform a tough job well. No wonder the nickname for
a smoke jumper is "Hotshot"!

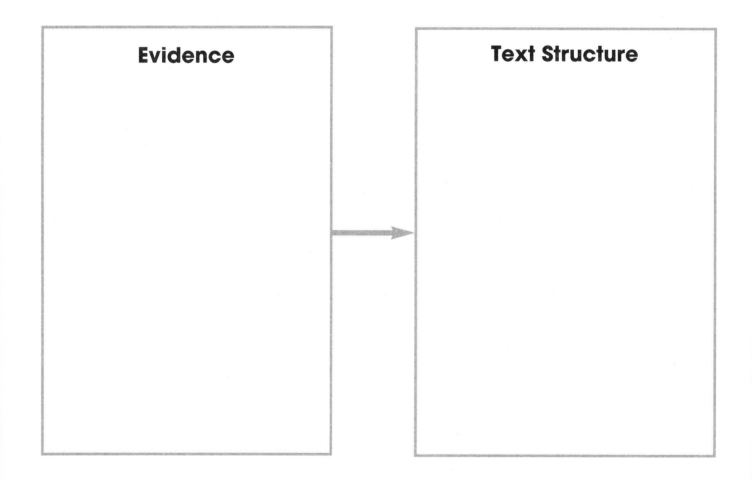

Evidence

Text Structure

Overview Using Text Features to Locate Information

Directions and Sample Answers for Activity Pages

Day 1	See "Provide a Real-World Example" below.
Day 2	Read and discuss the page. Then ask students to answer the questions. (**1:** *Earth: Fast Changes.* **2:** Erin Fry. **3:** page 2. **4:** page 20. **5:** Chapter 1. **6:** Responses will vary. **7:** Introduction and/or Conclusion. **8:** Responses will vary.)
Day 3	Read and discuss the page. Then ask students to color the circles in front of the best answers. (**1:** Thomas Edison. **2:** It's a Fact! **3:** to point to the photo that goes with the caption. **4:** A kinetograph is a movie camera. We see movies on TV. **5:** This man is filming a movie. **6:** What else did Thomas Edison invent?)
Day 4	Read and discuss the page. Then ask students to complete the sentences. (**1:** alphabetical. **2:** alphabetical. **3:** a five-sided shape. **4:** origami. **5:** 6 and 13–14. **6:** diamonds and squares. **7:** the same. **8:** making things by folding paper. **9:** Responses will vary.)
Day 5	Provide each student with a nonfiction book that includes a title page, table of contents, chapter headings, captions, sidebars, a glossary, and an index. Ask students to use the book to complete the chart. Afterward, meet individually with students to discuss their results. Use their responses to plan further instruction and review. (Responses will vary.)

Provide a Real-World Example

◆ Select a nonfiction book with a title page, table of contents, chapter headings, captions, sidebars, a glossary, and an index. Provide each student with a nonfiction book.

◆ Hand out the Day 1 activity page. **Say:** *Nonfiction books have certain text features. These features "tell" us information about the book. We can use these text features to locate, or find, information in the book.*

◆ Hold up your book. **Say:** *First, I will look at the title page. The title page shows the title and author of the book.* Point to the title and author's name as you read them aloud.

◆ **Say:** *Look at your book. Does your book have a title page? Then put a check mark in the* title page *box on your chart and write what the title page tells you.*

◆ Repeat the process for the remaining text features, first pointing one out in your book and then asking students to see if it is included in their books. Discuss their findings.

◆ **Say:** *This week we will learn more about these text features.* Write the following on chart paper:

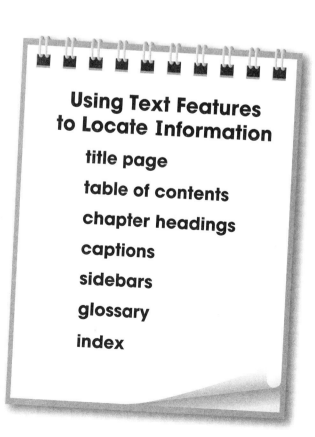

Using Text Features to Locate Information

title page

table of contents

chapter headings

captions

sidebars

glossary

index

Front to Back

Look at your book. Which features does it have? What does each feature "tell" you?

title page	
table of contents	
chapter headings	
captions	
sidebars	
glossary	
index	

Starting Out

Previewing the title page, table of contents, and chapter headings helps you get ready to read a book. In this book, the table of contents is on the title page. Read the page. Then answer the questions.

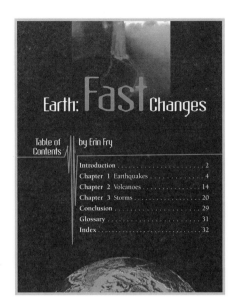

1. What is the title of the book?

   _____

2. Who is the author? _____

3. On what page will you begin reading the book? _____

4. What page would you go to if you want to learn about hurricanes? _____

5. Which chapter might tell about Earth's layers? _____

6. What is one thing you might read about in Chapter 2?

   _____

7. Where would you find information about the whole book? _____

8. What might be another good title for this book?

   _____

Captions and Sidebars

A caption tells more information about a picture. A sidebar tells more information about a topic. Read the following caption and sidebar from a book called *Great Inventions.* Then read the questions and color the circles in front of the best answers.

The next time you go to the movies, you can thank Thomas Edison. In 1890 he invented a movie camera, the kineto-graph which recorded movement on film for the first time.

This man is using a kinetograph.

It's a FACT!

Though TV is the most popular form of entertainment, few people know who invented it. His name was Philo T. Farnsworth, and he was only 20 years old!

1. Who is this page about?
○ Thomas Edison
○ people who go to movies

2. What is the sidebar heading?
○ Thomas Edison
○ It's a Fact!

3. Why does the page have an arrow?
○ to point to the photo that goes with the caption
○ to point to the photo that goes with the sidebar

4. How is the information in the caption related to the information in the sidebar?
○ Thomas Edison invented both the kinetograph and TV.
○ A kinetograph is a movie camera. We see movies on TV.

5. Which would be another good caption for the photo?
○ This man is Thomas Edison.
○ This man is filming a movie.

6. Which would be another good sidebar topic for this page?
○ What else did Thomas Edison invent?
○ What else did Philo T. Farnsworth invent?

Glossary and Index

A glossary defines key words in a book. The index shows where to find words. In this book, the glossary and index are on the same page. Read the page. Then complete the sentences.

●●●●●●●●●○●●●●●● Glossary ●●○●●●●●●●●●●●

diamond (DY-mund): a square turned so that one of
    its points is on the bottom

hexagon (HEK-suh-gahn): a shape with six sides

Japanese (ja-puh-NEEZ): from Japan

origami (or-ih-GAH-mee): the Japanese art of
    paper-folding

pentagon (PEN-tuh-gahn): a five-sided shape

polygon (PAH-lee-gahn): a closed shape with
    three or more sides

square (SKWAIR): a kind of rectangle with four
    right angles and four equal sides

triangle (TRY-an-gul): a shape with three sides
    and three corners

●●●●●●●●○●●●●●● Index ●●●●●●●●●○●●●

diamond 5	sides 6–7, 13
hexagon 7	square 5
Japanese 2–3	triangle 6, 13–14
pentagon 13	
polygon 13	

20

1. The words in the glossary are in _____ order.

2. The words in the index are in _____ order.

3. A pentagon is _____.

4. The Japanese art of paper folding is _____.

5. You can learn about triangles on pages _____.

6. On page 5, you can read about _____.

7. Some words in this glossary are _____ as the words in the index.

8. This book is probably about _____.

9. A good title for this book might be _____.

Assessment

Use your book to complete the chart.

	Page Number	One Thing I Learned
title page		
table of contents		
chapter heading		
caption		
sidebar		
glossary		
index		

   Unit 25 • Everyday Comprehension Intervention Activities Grade 5 • ©2010 Newmark Learning, LLC

Overview Using Graphic Features to Interpret Information

Directions and Sample Answers for Activity Pages

Day 1	See "Provide a Real-World Example" below.
Day 2	Discuss the time line and map. Then ask students to complete the sentences. (**Time line:** Kerma, Egypt, 1150 B.C., 250 B.C., kingdom, 350 A.D., city. **Map:** Egypt, Napata, Meroe, Nile River, 3rd, 1st.)
Day 3	Read and discuss the table and chart. Then ask students to complete the sentences. (**Table:** F0, strongest, F2, 73–112, F3, the information stays the same. **Chart:** Saturday, partly cloudy, Tuesday, Saturday/Sunday/Wednesday, Wednesday, the information may change.)
Day 4	Read and discuss the text and graph. Then ask students to circle the facts they learn from the graph. (People no longer got polio after about 1976. The highest number of polio cases was around 1953. More people had polio in 1950 than in 1960. The number of cases of polio dropped quickly after the Salk vaccine was available.)
Day 5	Provide each student with a nonfiction book that includes at least three of the graphic features on the list. Ask students to use the book to complete the chart. Afterward, meet individually with students to discuss their results. Use their responses to plan further instruction and review. (Responses will vary.)

Provide a Real-World Example

Using Graphic Features to Interpret Information
photographs
illustrations
labeled diagrams
time lines
maps
tables
charts
graphs

◆ Select a nonfiction book that has photographs, illustrations, and labeled diagrams. Provide each student with a nonfiction book.

◆ **Say:** *Nonfiction texts have graphic features. Readers must know how to interpret, or figure out, the information on a graphic feature. Pictures are one important type of graphic feature. Pictures can be photographs, illustrations, or labeled diagrams.*

◆ Share some photographs, illustrations, and labeled diagrams from your book. Discuss why the author used each one and what readers can learn from them. Then invite students to look through their own books and find photographs, illustrations, and labeled diagrams to share with the group.

◆ Hand out the Day 1 activity page. Discuss the pictures. Then ask students to color the circle in front of the reason the author used each one. (This chapter in the book is about multistory buildings. It is from long ago when people didn't have cameras. It shows parts we could not see in a photograph.)

◆ **Say:** *This week we will learn about some other graphic features, too.* Write the following on chart paper:

Pictures

Look at each picture. Then answer each question.

Why do you think the author used this photograph?

○ This chapter in the book is about schools.

○ This chapter in the book is about multistory buildings.

○ This chapter in the book is about shopping malls.

**Why do you think the author used this illustration
instead of a photograph?**

○ It shows something people imagined.

○ It shows parts we could not see in a photograph.

○ It is from long ago when people didn't have cameras.

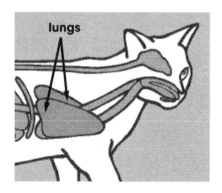

**Why do you think the author used this labeled diagram
instead of a photograph?**

○ It shows parts we could not see in a photograph.

○ It shows how cats are different from other types
of animals.

○ It shows the steps an animal's body goes through
to breathe in and out.

Time Lines and Maps

A time line tells when things happen. A map shows where things happen. This time line and map are from a book called *The Kingdom of Kush*. Complete the sentences about each graphic feature.

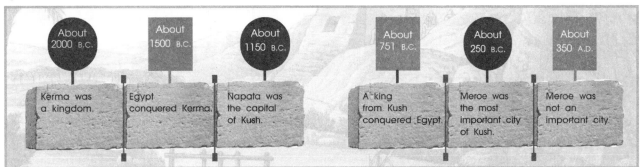

In about 1500 B.C., Egypt conquered _____, but in about 751 B.C., a

king from Kush conquered _____. Napata was the capital of

Kush in about _____, but Meroe was the most important city of Kush

in about _____. In about 2000 B.C., Kerma was a _____.

In about _____, Meroe was not an important _____.

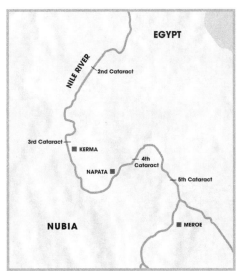

This is a map of Nubia. Nubia was an early river civilization in Africa. _____

was a civilization north of Nubia. Kerma was a city in Nubia. Two other cities were

_____ and _____. The _____ ran

through Nubia. The _____ Cataract was near Kerma. The _____

Cataract was nearest to the Red Sea.

Tables and Charts

A table shows information that stays the same in each column. A chart shows information that can change in one or more columns. This table and chart are from a book called *Weather and Storms*. Complete the sentences about each graphic feature.

Measuring the Power of a Tornado

The weakest tornado is the _____.

The F5 is the _____ tornado.

The _____ blows
at 113–157 miles per hour.

The F1 blows at _____ miles per hour.

A tornado that blows at 200 miles per hour is an

_____.

The Fujita Scale is a table instead of a chart because

_____.

The Fujita Scale	
Scale	**Wind Speed** miles per hour
F0	40–72
F1 **F2**	73–112 113–157
F3	158–206
F4 **F5**	207–260 261–318

 **Five-Day Weather Forecast**				
99° F / 76° F Clear	97° F / 74° F Clear	95° F / 72° F Partly Cloudy	92° F / 68° F Partly Cloudy	94° F / 68° F Clear
Saturday	Sunday	Monday	Tuesday	Wednesday

_____ will likely be the hottest day.

Monday and Tuesday will likely both be _____.

_____ will likely be cooler than Wednesday.

_____, _____, and _____ will likely
be clear. _____ will likely have the biggest difference between daytime
and nighttime temperatures.

The Five-Day Weather Forecast is a chart instead of a table because _____

_____.

Graphs

**A graph is a way to show how information is related. Look at the line graph.
Draw a circle around the facts you learn from the graph.**

Polio—United States 1940–1995

In the 1940s and 1950s, a disease called polio made thousands of people sick. Then, Jonas Salk created a vaccine that prevented polio. Several years later, people began taking a different polio vaccine orally (by mouth) instead of by an injection. However, Salk's vaccine is the only polio vaccine now used in the United States.

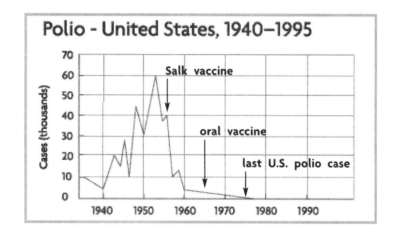

People no longer got polio as soon as the Salk vaccine was available.

People no longer got polio as soon as the oral vaccine was available.

People no longer got polio after about 1976.

The highest number of polio cases was around 1953.

The lowest number of polio cases was around 1940.

More people had polio in 1950 than in 1960.

The cases of polio went steadily up between 1940 and 1950.

The number of cases of polio dropped quickly after the Salk vaccine was available.

People still get polio in the United States today.

Assessment

Look at the list of graphic features.
Choose three that you find in your book.
Then complete the chart.

Graphic Features

photograph
illustration
labeled diagram
time line
map
table
chart
graph

Graphic Feature	Description	One Thing I Learned

Overview Distinguishing and Evaluating Fact and Opinion I

Directions and Sample Answers for Activity Pages

Day 1	See "Provide a Real-World Example" below.
Day 2	Read and discuss the passage. Then ask students to write **fact** or **opinion** after each statement. (**1:** opinion. **2:** fact. **3:** fact. **4:** opinion. **5:** fact. **6:** opinion.)
Day 3	Read and discuss the passage. Then ask students to write each sentence in the correct box. (**Facts:** 2, 3, 6. **Opinions:** 1, 4, 5.)
Day 4	Read and discuss the passage. Then ask students to circle **fact** or **opinion** for the statements. (**1:** opinion. **2:** fact. **3:** opinion. **4:** fact. **5:** fact. **6:** opinion.)
Day 5	Read the passage together. Ask students to record the facts, opinions, and evidence on their graphic organizers. Afterward, meet individually with students to discuss their results. Use their responses to plan further instruction and review. (**Facts:** serve it at Pizza Pizzazz on Fifth Street; has pineapple chunks, cheese, tomato sauce, green pepper, onion bits, peaches. **How I Know:** The writer can prove these statements true. **Opinions:** best pineapple pizza in the world, amazing, super delicious, fantastic, never want to eat any other kind of pizza. **How I Know:** The writer can't prove these statements true. Some people might disagree. The writer uses strong descriptive words such as **best** and **super**.)

Provide a Real-World Example

◆ Hand out the Day 1 activity page.

◆ **Say:** *Australia is the smallest continent. Everyone should visit Australia at least once. The first statement is a fact. I can prove this fact. No one can disagree with it. The second statement is an opinion. I would personally like to visit Australia, but some people might not.*

◆ Discuss ways you can prove facts. Encourage students to compare the sizes of all the continents on a map. Then discuss the word **everyone**.
Say: *Opinions often include all-inclusive words such as **all** or **nothing**, descriptive words such as **best** or **worst**, or belief words such as **should** or **shouldn't** that some people agree with and others do not.*

◆ Allow time for students to record the fact and opinion about Australia on their page. Then discuss the remaining statements and help students mark them as Fact or Opinion.

◆ Explain that students can also distinguish and evaluate fact and opinion when they read. Write the following on chart paper:

Distinguishing and Evaluating Fact and Opinion

A statement you can prove true is a fact.

You can prove a fact by personal observation or by relying on experts.

A statement you cannot prove true is an opinion.

An opinion includes words that tell or describe what someone believes.

Australia

**Listen. Complete the sentences below.
Then decide whether each statement is a fact or an opinion.**

Fact: Australia is the _____ continent.

Opinion: _____ should visit Australia at least once.

Australia is the most beautiful continent.	**Fact**	**Opinion**
Australia has kangaroos.	**Fact**	**Opinion**
Australia has mountains and a desert.	**Fact**	**Opinion**
Australia has excellent schools.	**Fact**	**Opinion**

The Harp

Read the passage. Then write *fact* or *opinion* after each statement.

The harp is a very old musical instrument. This instrument is such an important part of Irish history that it is a national symbol of Ireland. It's a perfect symbol for the country. One type of harp is the pedal harp. The pedal harp was invented in 1810. It has pedals that allow the harpist to change keys while playing. A pedal harp stands about 6 feet 2 inches tall and weighs around 75 pounds. It's an impressive-looking instrument. Some pedal harps have 47 strings. A harpist uses eight fingers to play the harp, and the sound it makes is heavenly. Maybe that's why some people say angels play harps!

1. The harp is a perfect symbol for the country of Ireland. _____

2. The pedal harp was invented in 1910. _____

3. A harpist can change keys while playing a pedal harp. _____

4. A pedal harp is an impressive-looking instrument. _____

5. A harpist uses eight fingers to play up to 47 strings. _____

6. A pedal harp makes a heavenly sound. _____

Name _____

Row, Row, Row Your Boat

**Read the passage. Then write each sentence in the
correct box.**

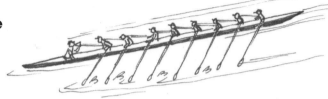

Some people row boats for fun or to go from
place to place. Other people compete in rowing
races. Rowing competitions are the most exciting kind of boat racing to watch.
The sport of racing in high school and college is known as "crew." The boats in
this sport are called shells. A shell is a long, slim, good-looking boat. The rowing
team sits in the shell on sliding seats, which allow them to push back with their
legs on each stroke. Team members may row with one or two oars. In sweep rowing,
a rower pulls one oar with both hands. In sculling, a rower pulls two oars, an oar in
each hand. Only physically fit people should try rowing!

1. Rowing shells are good-looking boats.
2. Sweep rowers sit on sliding seats.
3. In crew, rowers use their legs as well as their arms.
4. Rowing competitions are exciting to watch.
5. You should not row if you're not physically fit.
6. A scull rower pulls two oars.

Facts	Opinions

A Fearsome Hunter

Read the passage. Then circle *fact* or *opinion* for each statement.

Living mainly in the rivers of Africa and the Amazon is a fish you don't want to see—the piranha. Piranhas vary in color. They may be green, gray, or bluish black. The piranha is an ugly fish with a huge mouth and razor-like teeth. It weighs less than three pounds, but it attacks animals many times its size. Its teeth and powerful jaw muscles make it a fearsome hunter. Piranhas live and hunt in huge packs called shoals. A piranha's appetite is ravenous. Its usual prey consists of fish, birds, and small mammals, but it will also eat humans and cattle if given the opportunity. Beware of the piranha, for it's the most dangerous creature in the water!

1. You don't want to see a piranha.   fact   opinion

2. A piranha may be green, gray, or bluish black.   fact   opinion

3. A piranha is an ugly fish.   fact   opinion

4. A piranha will attack an animal many times its size.   fact   opinion

5. Most piranhas eat fish, birds, and small mammals.   fact   opinion

6. A piranha is the most dangerous creature in the water.   fact   opinion

Name _____

Assessment

**Read the e-mail. Write the facts and how you know they're facts.
Then write the opinions and how you know they're opinions.**

Hi, Nora!
I had to e-mail you right away. I just ate the best pineapple
pizza in the world! They serve it at Pizza Pizzazz on Fifth
Street. I've had pineapple pizza before, but this one was
amazing! It had the usual pineapple chunks, cheese, and
tomato sauce on it. But it also had slices of green pepper and
little onion bits—plus a surprise ingredient that made it super
delicious. Guess what it was? Peaches! Maybe this pizza
sounds crazy to you, but it's fantastic! You'll have to try it
when we get together next week. YOU WILL NEVER WANT
TO EAT ANY OTHER KIND OF PIZZA!
Deb

Facts	**How I Know**

Opinions	**How I Know**

Overview Distinguishing and Evaluating Fact and Opinion II

Directions and Sample Answers for Activity Pages

Day 1	See "Provide a Real-World Example" below.
Day 2	Read and discuss the passage. Then ask students to write facts and opinions about storm chasing and to circle signal words. (**Facts:** A tornado is a powerful, funnel-shaped storm. An experienced tour guide takes you to Tornado Alley, where most tornadoes occur. This region includes most of the midwestern states. You ride in a radar-equipped chase vehicle with a global positioning computer system. After your guide locates the storm, you drive to that location to observe and collect data. **Opinions:** Chasing tornadoes is thrilling. There is nothing to be nervous about. Storm chasing is a great way to spend a vacation. **Signal Words: thrilling, nervous, great.**)
Day 3	Read and discuss the passage. Then ask students to write each sentence in the correct box. (**Facts:** 1, 3, 4. **Opinions:** 2, 5, 6.)
Day 4	Read and discuss the passage. Then ask students to circle **fact** or **opinion** for the statements. (**1:** fact. **2:** fact. **3:** opinion. **4:** fact. **5:** fact. **6:** opinion. **7:** opinion. **8:** fact.)
Day 5	Read the passage together. Ask students to record the facts, opinions, and evidence on their graphic organizers. Afterward, meet individually with students to discuss their results. Use their responses to plan further instruction and review. (**Facts:** on the California coast; oldest have lived for thousands of years; average 375 feet tall; diameters of 20 feet; soft, thick, reddish-brown bark; not harmed by insects and fungi; sometimes injured or killed by fire; fires have gutted bases of several huge trees; two or three people can stand inside. **How I Know:** The author can prove these statements true through personal observation or research. **Opinions:** remember them for the rest of your life; magnificent trees; breathtaking sight; bark is stunning. **How I Know:** The author can't prove these statements true. Some people might disagree with them. The author uses words such as **magnificent, breathtaking,** and **stunning.**)

Provide a Real-World Example

◆ Hand out the Day 1 activity page.

◆ **Say:** *This page has facts and opinions about piano lessons. You can prove a fact through personal observation or by relying on experts. No one can disagree with a fact. An opinion is something someone personally believes. People can give reasons to back up their opinions, but other people might disagree with them. Opinions often include all-inclusive words such as **everything** or **never**, descriptive words such as **greatest** or **worst**, or belief words such as **should** or **shouldn't** that some people agree with and others do not.*

◆ Ask students to work with a partner to label each statement as a fact or opinion. (fact, fact, opinion, opinion, fact, opinion, opinion, fact) Encourage them to circle words that signal an opinion. Then, invite the partnerships to share and defend their answers for the group.

◆ Remind students that they can also distinguish and evaluate fact and opinion when they read a passage. Review the chart created in the previous unit:

Distinguishing and Evaluating Fact and Opinion

A statement you can prove true is a fact.

You can prove a fact by personal observation or by relying on experts.

A statement you cannot prove true is an opinion.

An opinion includes words that tell or describe what someone believes.

Name _____

Piano Lessons

**Listen. Complete the sentences below.
Then decide whether each statement is a fact or an opinion.**

Many kids take piano lessons.

_____

It is hard to find a piano teacher
in some communities.

_____

Adults enjoy music more if they took
piano lessons as a child.

_____

The piano is an easy instrument to learn to play.

_____

Pianos come in different shapes, sizes, and colors.

_____

Piano teachers should have recitals
at least once a year.

_____

Piano students shouldn't have to
practice on weekends.

_____

Learning to play the piano helps some people
learn to play other instruments more easily.

_____

Chasing Storms

Read the passage. Then follow the directions.

Have you ever wished you could see a powerful, funnel-shaped storm up close? Are you brave enough to stand in violent winds under a greenish-black sky? If you answered *yes* and *yes*, then you might consider joining a tornado-chasing tour. Chasing tornadoes is thrilling! An experienced tour guide takes you to Tornado Alley, where most tornadoes occur. This region includes most of the midwestern states. There is nothing to be nervous about! You ride in a radar-equipped chase vehicle with a global positioning computer system. After your guide locates the storm, you drive to that location to observe and collect data. Storm chasing is a great way to spend a vacation!

Write three facts about storm chasing.

1. _____

2. _____

3. _____

Write three opinions about storm chasing.
Then circle the descriptive words that signal an opinion.

1. _____

2. _____

3. _____

Clowning Around

Read the passage. Then write each sentence in the correct box.

Being a clown is an easy way to make a living. Those interested in becoming a clown can go to a clown school. Many clown schools offer classes in juggling, riding a unicycle, and walking on stilts. These are the most important classes. At some clown schools, clowns-to-be can take a class in slaps and falls as well as pantomime and dance classes. But learning to create a clown character is really the most fun. Clown students experiment with makeup, costumes, and props to come up with their own clown personality. Each clown has a unique appearance and character traits, but the main job of all clowns is to make people feel good.

1. Clowns-to-be can learn to pantomime and dance.
2. Creating a character is the most fun part of becoming a clown.
3. People can go to clown school.
4. Clowns can use makeup, costumes, and props.
5. Juggling is one of the most important classes at clown school.
6. Being a clown is an easy way to make a living.

Facts	Opinions

Hairy Mammoths

**Read the passage. Then circle *fact* or
opinion for each statement.**

The hairy mammoth, an elephant-like
animal that stood twelve feet tall and
weighed up to 15,000 pounds, was hunted
by early man. Packs of nasty wolves were probably the only other danger to an adult
mammoth. Hairy mammoths lived in Earth's Arctic region. As a result, the animals had a
lot of fat as well as a long, hairy coat to survive the frigid climate. They also had small
ears, whereas modern elephants have large, funny-looking ears. The tusks of the hairy
mammoth were extremely long, up to sixteen feet in length. Like today's elephants, hairy
mammoths were social animals. Female mammoths were good mothers who took care of
their young for long periods of time.

1. The hairy mammoth had enemies.	fact	opinion
2. Some hairy mammoths weighed 15,000 pounds.	fact	opinion
3. The wolves in the Arctic region were nasty.	fact	opinion
4. Some hairy mammoths had tusks that were sixteen feet long.	fact	opinion
5. Hairy mammoths were social animals.	fact	opinion
6. Female mammoths were good mothers.	fact	opinion
7. Modern elephants have funny-looking ears.	fact	opinion
8. Hairy mammoths had a lot of fat to help them keep warm.	fact	opinion

Assessment

**Read the passage. Write the facts and how you know they're facts.
Then write the opinions and how you know they're opinions.**

If you see the giant redwood trees on the California coast, you will remember them for the rest of your life. The oldest giants have lived for thousands of years. On average, redwoods are 375 feet tall, and some have diameters of 20 feet. These magnificent trees are a breathtaking sight! The redwood tree has a soft, thick, reddish-brown bark. On a young tree, this bark is stunning. Although insects and fungi do not harm redwoods, fire sometimes injures or kills young trees. Fires have also gutted the bases of several huge trees, leaving hollows so large that two or three people can stand inside.

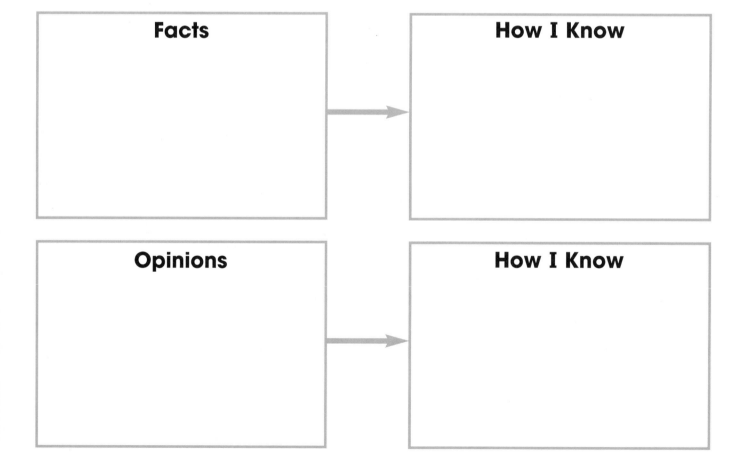

Facts		How I Know
	→	

Opinions		How I Know
	→	

Overview Making Judgments I

Directions and Sample Answers for Activity Pages

Day 1	See "Provide a Real-World Example" below.
Day 2	Read and discuss the passage. Then ask students to complete the sentences. (**Author's Judgment:** Kids should be allowed to watch TV as long as parents set rules. **1:** one or two. **2:** homework, chores. **3:** positive, educational. **4:** appropriate. **5:** physical activities, socializing, leisure reading, and hobbies. **6:** topics, school.)
Day 3	Read and discuss the passage. Then ask students to circle the best word choice for each sentence. (**1:** better than lawn mowers. **2:** should not. **3:** New businesses. **4:** Animals. **5:** care. **6:** does not approve.)
Day 4	Read and discuss the passage. Then ask students to color the circles in front of the best answers. (**1:** The bird on the video was not an ivory-billed woodpecker. **2:** A blue jay's call is similar to an ivory-billed woodpecker's call. No one had seen an ivory-billed woodpecker for more than sixty years. A pileated woodpecker looks a lot like an ivory-billed woodpecker. It was impossible to identify the bird from the brief, blurry video. A pileated woodpecker makes the same double-pecking knock as an ivory-billed woodpecker.)
Day 5	Read the passage together. Ask students to record the evidence and author's judgment on their graphic organizers. Afterward, meet individually with students to discuss their results. Use their responses to plan further instruction and review. (**Evidence:** You can eat arracacha in place of potatoes. It's an excellent source of calcium. If you eat a lot of arracacha, your skin will turn yellow. Arracacha plants can get viruses. I like potatoes a lot, and I get calcium from milk. **Author's Judgment:** Potatoes and milk are better than arracacha.)

Provide a Real-World Example

◆ Hand out the Day 1 activity page.

◆ **Say:** *Different schools have different rules. In some schools, students are not allowed to talk in the halls. What are some reasons a school might have this rule?* Allow time for students to discuss and record their ideas in the first column of the chart.

◆ **Say:** *In other schools, students are allowed to talk in the halls. What are some reasons a school might have this rule?* Allow time for students to discuss and record their ideas in the second column of the chart.

◆ Discuss which rule applies to your school. **Say:** *The school leaders talked about both rules. They used the evidence to make a judgment. They felt that the evidence for one rule was stronger than the evidence for the other rule.* Then explain that authors sometimes make judgments, too. Write the following on chart paper:

Making Judgments

Look for two sides of an issue.

Look at the evidence for both sides.

Look for words that show the author has chosen one side over the other.

Decide if you agree with the author's decision.

Name _____

In the Hall

List the reasons for each rule. Then weigh the evidence and make your judgment.

Reasons to ask students to be quiet in the halls	**Reasons to allow students to talk in the halls**

My Judgment: _____

_____

Unit 29 • Everyday Comprehension Intervention Activities Grade 5 • ©2010 Newmark Learning, LLC

Watching TV

Read the passage. Then complete the sentences.

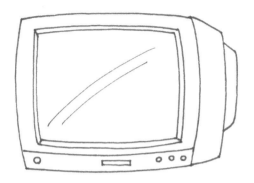

    Some parents do not allow their children to watch TV. They feel that many fictional programs are too violent and many reality programs are inappropriate. These parents are also aware of research that says kids who watch too much TV do poorly in school, have no interest in leisure reading or hobbies, don't socialize with others, and don't participate in physical activities.

    But what about the benefits of watching TV? Parents can set some rules that allow their children to watch TV without ill effects. For example, some parents limit TV to one or two hours a day after homework and chores are finished. In addition, they help their children select positive, educational programs that are appropriate for their age. This still leaves time for physical activities, socializing, leisure reading, and hobbies—and can even support topics students are learning about in school. Why not let kids have the best of both worlds?

Author's Judgment:

Kids _____ be allowed to watch TV as long as parents set _____.

Evidence Supporting Author's Judgment:

1. Parents can limit TV to _____ hours per day.

2. Students can finish their _____ and _____ before

    watching TV.

3. Parents can help their children select _____ programs.

4. Parents can help their children select programs that are _____

    for their age.

5. With these rules, kids will still have time for _____.

6. Some TV shows even support _____ students are learning

    about in _____.

Animals or Machines?

Read the passage. Then draw a circle around the best word choice for each sentence.

Instead of mowing large areas of grass on their properties, some companies are now renting goats to eat the grass. Yes, goats have become lawn mowers! New businesses are providing the goats. Sometimes as many as 200 goats will stay for a week and chew away. Those who hire the goats say the animals are better for the environment than gas-consuming lawn mowers. Goats aren't noisy, and they don't pollute the air. Besides, many employees think the goats are cute!

Cuteness aside, what about the well-being of the goats? Animals that are part of a business often suffer. For example, the goats may not get enough shade and water on hot days. If the weather is stormy, they may have to keep "working" instead of finding shelter. During their stay, the goats' housing may be inadequate. And will they receive veterinary care? Goats are animals—not machines!

1. Some companies feel that goats are (as good as lawn mowers, better than lawn mowers).

2. Other people feel that goats (should, should not) have to work for a living.

3. (New businesses, People who hire goats) provide as many as 200 goats to eat grass on a property.

4. (Animals, Lawn mowers) require special attention on hot or stormy days.

5. People who hire goats (care, do not care) about the environment.

6. From the evidence, it appears that the author (approves, does not approve) of using goats as lawn mowers.

Unit 29 • *Everyday Comprehension Intervention Activities Grade 5* • ©2010 Newmark Learning, LLC

The Ivory-Billed Woodpecker

Read the passage. Then read the questions and color the circles in front of the best answers.

It was exciting news! In 2004, someone in Arkansas reported seeing an ivory-billed woodpecker. Ornithologists, scientists who study birds, thought this bird was extinct, as no one had seen one since the 1940s. Several respected ornithologists looked at a videotape of the bird and listened to bird sounds recorded in the area. They believed the calls were those of an ivory-bill as were the double-pecking knocks. They announced that the ivory-billed woodpecker lives. Other respected scientists were not so sure. They felt the bird was a pileated woodpecker. It greatly resembles the ivory-bill and makes the same double knocks. They said the calls could be those of a blue jay. They also pointed out that the video was brief and blurry, making a positive identification impossible. My question is this: If ivory-billed woodpeckers really were still alive, why had there been no sightings for more than sixty years?

1. What is the author's judgment about the ivory-billed woodpecker?
○ The bird on the video was an ivory-billed woodpecker.
○ The bird on the video was not an ivory-billed woodpecker.
○ Ornithologists should get better videos before trying to identify birds.

2. What pieces of evidence support the author's judgment?
○ A blue jay's call is similar to an ivory-billed woodpecker's call.
○ Ornithologists are scientists who study birds.
○ No one had seen an ivory-billed woodpecker for more than sixty years.
○ Ornithologists listened to bird sounds recorded in the area.
○ A pileated woodpecker looks a lot like an ivory-billed woodpecker.
○ The bird on the video made a double-pecking knock.
○ It was impossible to identify the bird from the brief, blurry video.
○ Someone in Arkansas reported seeing an ivory-billed woodpecker.
○ A pileated woodpecker makes the same double-pecking knock as an ivory-billed woodpecker.

Assessment

Read the letter. Then write the evidence and author's judgment in the boxes.

Dear Grandma,

Since you plant a vegetable garden every summer, I thought you'd like to hear about something we learned in school today. Arracacha is a popular vegetable grown in South America. It's a root vegetable and starchy. You can eat it in place of potatoes. You don't eat an arracacha root raw, but cooked arracacha is supposed to have a unique flavor that's tastier than potatoes. The article we read said that arracacha has a pleasing aroma while cooking and an appetizing color. Plus, it's an excellent source of calcium (for kids' bones, you know)—four times better than a potato. Sounds good, huh? But then we found out that if you eat a lot of arracacha, your skin will turn yellow! The other bad news is that the arracacha plants can get viruses. Anyway, I like potatoes a lot, and I get calcium from milk, so I think I'll stick with those!

Love,

Lacey

Evidence	**Author's Judgment**

Overview Making Judgments II

Directions and Sample Answers for Activity Pages

Day 1	See "Provide a Real-World Example" below.
Day 2	Read and discuss the passage. Then ask students to circle the author's judgment, underline the evidence, and complete the sentence. (**Judgment:** Solar panels may be our best option in our quest to preserve Earth's dwindling supply of fossil fuels. **Evidence:** quiet, produce no pollution, electricity is free, produce energy on overcast days, eliminating any space problems, less expensive than running electrical wires. **Sentence:** Responses will vary.)
Day 3	Read and discuss the passage. Then ask students to circle the author's judgment and answer the questions. (**Author's Judgment:** As long as zoo designers and workers respect animals' needs and rights, zoos should exist for the good they do. **1:** spaces that are too small, belong in the wild, stressed, incompetent zookeepers, poor conditions. **2:** do not confine animals to cages; spacious with natural habitats; places of education; protect and raise endangered species. **3:** Responses will vary. **4:** Responses will vary.)
Day 4	Read and discuss the passage. Then ask students to color the circles in front of the best answers. (**1:** Downhill skiing can be a safe sport. **2:** Proper clothing and equipment help you to be a smart skier. **3:** Many people don't ski courses suited to their ability levels. **My Judgment:** Responses will vary.)
Day 5	Read the passage together. Ask students to record the evidence and their own judgment on their graphic organizers. Afterward, meet individually with students to discuss their results. Use their responses to plan further instruction and review. (**Evidence:** Answers will vary but should be based on information in the passage. **My Judgment:** Responses will vary.)

Provide a Real-World Example

◆ Hand out the Day 1 activity page.

◆ **Say:** *Some people use old rags when they clean their houses and cars. These people feel that using paper towels is wasteful. What are some ways that using paper towels is wasteful?* Allow time for students to discuss and record their ideas in the first column of the chart.

◆ **Say:** *Other people feel that using cleaning rags is wasteful. For example, people must put the dirty rags in the washing machine, which requires extra water and electricity.* Allow time for students to discuss and record this concept in the second column of the chart.

◆ **Say:** *Think about the evidence. Write your judgment on the line. Then share your judgment with a partner, including the evidence that most supports your judgment.*

◆ Remind students that authors sometimes make judgments, too. Review the chart created in the previous unit:

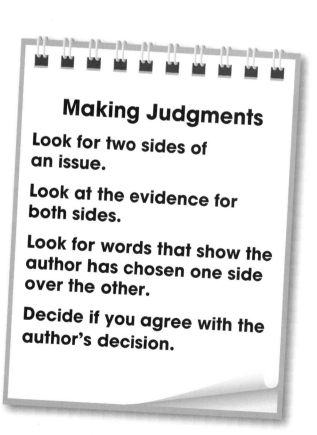

Making Judgments

Look for two sides of an issue.

Look at the evidence for both sides.

Look for words that show the author has chosen one side over the other.

Decide if you agree with the author's decision.

Cleaning Day

List the problems for each item. Then weigh the evidence and make your judgment.

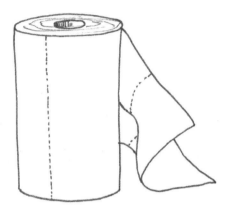   

Problems with paper towels	Problems with reusable cleaning rags

My Judgment:

_____

_____

_____

Solar Panels

**Read the passage. Draw a circle around the author's judgment.
Then underline the evidence that supports the author's judgment.**

    Some people get their electricity from solar panels. Solar panels are quiet and produce
no pollution. Installing solar panels is costly, but once they're installed, the electricity is
free. In the past, solar panels were ineffective on days with little sunshine. However,
new technologies are helping solar panels produce energy on overcast days. Solar panels
are often installed on rooftops, eliminating any space problems. In isolated locations,
installing solar panels is less expensive than running electrical wires. Solar panels may
be our best option in our quest to preserve Earth's dwindling supply of fossil fuels.

Complete this sentence.

I (agree, do not agree) with the author's judgment, because _____

_____

_____.

Name _____

Should We Have Zoos?

**Read the passage. Draw a circle around
the author's judgment. Then answer the questions.**

Some people believe that zoos confine animals
to spaces that are too small. These people believe
that the animals belong in the wild. They feel that
the animals are stressed by living in zoos. They also
cite examples of incompetent zookeepers and poor
conditions as proof that zoos should be closed. But should all zoos be shut down because
of the few bad ones? Many zoos do not confine animals to cages. These zoos are spacious
with natural habitats for the animals. Whereas zoos used to exist solely for entertainment,
many zoos today are places of education. Children and adults alike learn about nature,
habitats, ecology, and endangered animals. Many modern zoos strive to protect and raise
endangered species. As long as zoo designers and workers respect animals' needs and
rights, zoos should exist for the good they do.

1. What evidence does the author giving for closing zoos?

_____

_____

2. What evidence does the author give for keeping zoos open?

_____

_____

**3. Do you think most people will agree with the author's judgment?
Why or why not?**

_____

_____

4. Do you agree with the author's judgment? Why or why not?

_____

_____

Downhill Skiing

Read the passage. Read the questions and color the circles in front of the best answers. Then write your judgment.

    Downhill skiing can be a dangerous sport. Skiers who lose control can suffer serious harm, including broken bones or head injuries. However, many people find skiing an exhilarating outdoor activity. The key is to be a smart skier. Get the proper clothing and equipment. Wear a helmet. Take some lessons from an experienced skier or even a professional. Let him or her help you choose a course suited to your ability level. Finally, know when to quit for the day. A tired skier is likely to suffer an accident. Skiing can be a safe, fun family adventure . . . not to mention the breathtaking views and delicious hot chocolate that ski resorts provide!

1. What judgment does the author make?

  ◯ Families should take their vacations at a ski resort.

  ◯ Downhill skiing is dangerous for nonprofessionals.

  ◯ Downhill skiing can be a safe sport.

2. What is one piece of evidence the author uses for making this judgment?

  ◯ Proper clothing and equipment help you to be a smart skier.

  ◯ Skiing is so exhilarating that many people ski for hours.

  ◯ Broken bones usually heal in time.

3. Why might some people disagree with the author's judgment?

  ◯ Many people don't ski courses suited to their ability levels.

  ◯ Experienced skiers seldom lose control.

  ◯ Wearing a helmet helps a skier stay safe.

My Judgment:

_____

_____

_____

Assessment

Read the passage. Then write the evidence and a judgment in the boxes.

Walk-in medical clinics are popping up across the United States. Some medical organizations don't approve of them. They point out that the nurse practitioners who work in the clinics don't know the patients' medical histories. Since they aren't doctors, they may not recognize a serious medical condition. These organizations feel that each clinic needs a physician's supervision. They also stress the importance of regular inspections to verify that the site meets health codes.

Other people think the walk-in clinics are a good idea. The hours and locations are convenient The clinics are in pharmacies, supermarkets, and discount stores and are open late seven days a week. Many people also like the immediate care they offer. Nurse practitioners can give flu shots and treat minor conditions such as ear infections and sore throats. Often, busy doctors can't see a person right away, and going to a hospital emergency room results in a long wait.

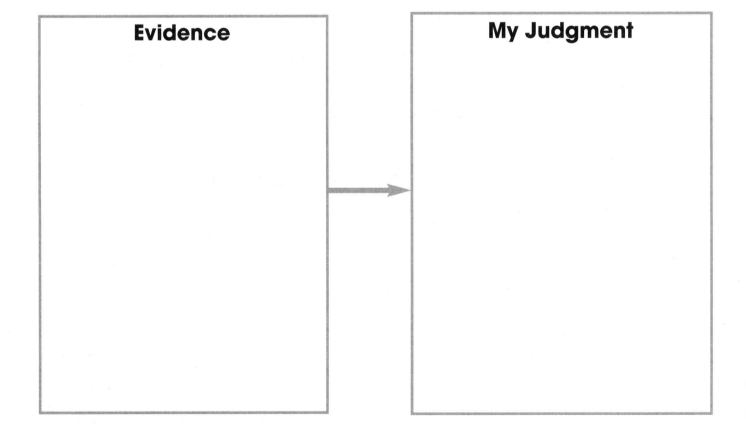

Evidence	**My Judgment**

Notes

Notes

Notes

Notes

Notes

Notes